PIRKAY AVOS ON MARRIAGE

Pirkay Avos on Marriage

Timely Messages from
a Timeless Source

Rabbi Reuven P. Bulka, C.M.

KTAV PUBLISHING HOUSE

For the Generated Generations
That Are Now Generating Generations

Yisroel Meir & Miriam Shonek

Dovid Nisson & Tova Shonek

Fraidy & Shmuel Clinton

Rochel Leah & Menachem Yehoshua Greenwald

Yeshaya & Tzippora Leah Shonek

Rikki & Daniel Ash

Ruti & Yona Epstein

Kayla & Yosef Marx

Contents

Introduction

Pirkay Avos, literally "Chapters of the Elders," is Jewish ethics in its most profound expression. It deals with the way we interact with our fellows, and proffers more than just good advice. Pirkay Avos is clear direction on the right way to behave in our dealings with others.

It is therefore not a stretch at all to look to Pirkay Avos as a wellspring of direction for how to relate to one's spouse. Admittedly, not every Mishnah statement can be easily applied to the marital sphere, but the inherent messages in most, if not all of the Mishnah statements, can be applied to marriage, some more easily so than others.

There is little doubt that if we live by the guidelines of Pirkay Avos, we will significantly improve the quality of our interpersonal relations.

There is likewise little doubt that if we employ Pirkay Avos as the constitution for husband-wife interaction, we will significantly enhance the quality of marriage in general, and individual marriages in particular.

For an understanding of Pirkay Avos from a psychological perspective, and in a way which connects each Mishnah with the preceding and following Mishnah statements, in a thematic approach, see my book, *Chapters of the Sages*, first published by Feldheim in 1980, later by Jason Aronson in 1993, and in 2002 as part of the Jason Aronson Jewish Classics series. The original title of that book was *As a Tree by the Waters*.

This volume enlarges upon that book, offering insights to help marriage move from ordinary to extraordinary, from good to great, from perfunctory to purposeful.

This volume was written in two stages. I started writing it many years ago, but other matters got in the way, or maybe I let other matters get in the way. Perhaps in the back of my mind I did not think that the marriage theme would carry through for all of Pirkay Avos.

Then came COVID-19 in early 2020, around Purim of 5780. In spite of the many new obligations necessitated by this pandemic, I no longer had the excuse of "not enough time in the day."

The time was there for the taking, and I was left with no choice but to try finishing the book.

So, I was able to finish in the COVID-19 summer. I am grateful to the many people who pressed me on what I was writing, forcing me to fess up, and to stop procrastinating.

Special thanks to my super grandson and computer guru, Avi Bulka, who always had time and insight to address problems, of which there were many, including at least twice when significant patches of the book were lost, and he "found" them.

Few things are more disheartening to an author than losing part of a manuscript. Getting up from the floor, so to say, to start again, is not easily achieved. Avi saved me from that. In fact, the joy of his recovering the lost pages energized me to finish even more quickly.

As if this was not enough, when there were serious edits in the final stages, including in the Hebrew, before the final send off to the publisher, Avi was here, as usual, to help with the finishing touches. My gratitude to Avi, and my appreciation, know no bounds.

My dear son Eliezer, himself a computer whiz, was his usual helpful self, offering assistance, insights and advice that significantly enhanced this volume. Thanks to my dear son Rav Binyomin, for his timely and helpful ideas. Special kudos to my dear wife Leah, for her insightful suggestions for the front cover, and appreciation to my dear granddaughter Rikki Ash for her helpful recommendations.

I am deeply grateful to Moshe Heller of Ktav, who continues to be most supportive and encouraging. Thanks also to Raphaël Freeman for his usual masterful job making the volume so readable. And special appreciation to Shira Atwood at Ktav for her gracious helpfulness.

In closing, I share with you an important observation. The Jewish marriage ceremony seems quite perfunctory, even legalistic. It is a fusion of assuming obligation and bestowing blessing.

The couple undertake to fulfill their marital duties, and the community invokes the blessing of God that they succeed in their sacred agreement.

Pirkay Avos on Marriage presents a full picture of what these duties entail. There are many themes that emerge from this study, and some that are recurring themes throughout the volume.

May this volume achieve its primary purpose, as previously enunciated – to enhance and uplift marriage in general, and each marriage in particular.

Rabbi Reuven P. Bulka, C.M.
Ottawa, Ontario, Canada
Summer, 2020

Pirkay Avos on Marriage

Prologue

כָּל יִשְׂרָאֵל יֵשׁ לָהֶם חֵלֶק לְעוֹלָם הַבָּא, שֶׁנֶּאֱמַר: וְעַמֵּךְ כֻּלָּם צַדִּיקִים לְעוֹלָם
יִירְשׁוּ אָרֶץ נֵצֶר מַטָּעַי מַעֲשֵׂה יָדַי לְהִתְפָּאֵר.

All Israel has a share in the world-to-come, as it is said: "And Your people,
all righteous, shall inherit the land forever, the branch of My plantings, the
work of My hands, to glorify Me." (YESHAYAHU 60:21).

This prologue is technically not a part of Pirkay Avos, but is the preamble to the regular recitation of this illuminating treatise in the period between Pesah and Rosh HaShanah.

In other words, it serves as a tone-setter. The basic message of this prologue is that we all begin life with some real estate in the world-to-come.

This is God's vote of confidence in us that we can have meaningful lives worthy of eternal blessing.

We do not start off with a negative balance, embarking on a life wherein we must first clear up the deficit. There are more precise and damning terms to describe this negativity, but whatever we call it, this prologue is a categorical rejection of that notion.

We are not doomed and in need of salvation; instead we begin life with reservations in the future world. It is up to us to assure we do not lose those reservations. This we achieve by living worthy lives.

On the one hand, living a worthy life seems like a daunting task. On the other hand, we have God's confidence that we can do it. Otherwise, God would not have reserved our places.

Pirkay Avos on marriage might appear as too high a mountain to climb, but it is within our capacity to reach the summit.

So, every time we initiate the Pirkay Avos Shabbos reading, we start with a powerful statement which, in a most subtle yet penetrating way, says – you can do it.

We can do it, we can achieve wonderful, exemplary marital unions.

As to how we can achieve this, we will let Pirkay Avos speak and inspire.

Chapter One

א. מֹשֶׁה קִבֵּל תּוֹרָה מִסִּינַי וּמְסָרָהּ לִיהוֹשֻׁעַ, וִיהוֹשֻׁעַ לִזְקֵנִים, וּזְקֵנִים
לִנְבִיאִים, וּנְבִיאִים מְסָרוּהָ לְאַנְשֵׁי כְנֶסֶת הַגְּדוֹלָה. הֵם אָמְרוּ שְׁלֹשָׁה דְבָרִים:
הֱווּ מְתוּנִים בַּדִּין, וְהַעֲמִידוּ תַלְמִידִים הַרְבֵּה, וַעֲשׂוּ סְיָג לַתּוֹרָה.

*Moshe received the Torah from Sinai and transmitted it to Yehoshua, and
Yehoshua to the elders, the Elders to the Prophets, and the Prophets transmitted the Torah to the Men of the Great Assembly. They (the Men of the
Great Assembly) emphasized three things — be cautious in judgment, raise
up many students, and make a fence around the Torah.*

The fact that Pirkay Avos begins with the chain of transmission ema-
nating from Sinai is an eloquent way of saying that the insights being
shared herein are informed by our tradition, and have stood the test
of time.

Therefore, what is contained herein is at once timely and timeless.

Although the statement that we *be cautious in judgment* deals
essentially with the judicial process, it can easily be applied to daily
life, and to married life.

There are times in marriage when matters do not unfold to our
liking, or when we do not like the actions of our spouse. The meal is
not ready on time, the spouse is not responsive enough to a request,
or the spouse is not behaving in a sensitive manner.

A small or large incident leads to a general conclusion about the
other, and the downward spiral begins. We are urged not to rush to
judgment, and instead to first fully understand the behavior of the
husband or wife.

Again, the imperative to *raise up many students* is not a marriage related directive, but has implications for marriage. We are all encouraged to be good examples, good teachers, good role models; in what we teach, in the example we set.

The example we set and the atmosphere we create in the home, as husband and wife – the tranquility of the home, can be a most inspirational model for our children, our families, and their friends, a model which they can implement as they set out to build their own homes.

A life lived according to Torah dictates is a life governed by precise and exact prescription. One can suffice with merely staying with the prescription, adhering to the letter of the law, but going no further.

A fence around the Torah, much like a fence around property, serves to protect, to assure that there is no trespass of the property, or trespass of the Torah. The Torah is so important that we build effective and well thought out hedges. The fence speaks volumes about the importance we attach to the Torah.

We can, and should do the same with marriage; to devise strategies to assure that the marriage continues to thrive. These include enactments made by the couple together, or individually, where they sense greatest vulnerability.

To protect against not giving each other proper attention, a fence would be to set up a time, once a day, or once a week, whatever works, a quiet time when no disturbance or interruption short of emergency is allowed, when the couple talk to each other.

There are a host of other potential fences, to guard against personal or interactional habits impacting negatively on the marriage.

Doing this will help make the marriage more exemplary for the many students, and will help avoid the rush to judgment that may harm the relationship.

❧ MISHNAH 2 ❧

ב. שִׁמְעוֹן הַצַּדִּיק הָיָה מִשְׁיָרֵי כְנֶסֶת הַגְּדוֹלָה. הוּא הָיָה אוֹמֵר: עַל שְׁלֹשָׁה דְבָרִים הָעוֹלָם עוֹמֵד – עַל הַתּוֹרָה, וְעַל הָעֲבוֹדָה, וְעַל גְּמִילוּת חֲסָדִים.

Shimon the Righteous was one of the last survivors of the Great Assembly. He used to say: The world stands on three things – on the Torah, on the sacred service, and on the practice of loving-kindness.

It is not at all a stretch to suggest that the world of marriage stands on these pillars – on the Torah, on the sacred service, and on the practice of loving-kindness.

The *Torah* is what God has given to us, *sacred service* is what we give to God, and *loving-kindness* is what we give to each other.

The Torah is our guide for everyday behavior, a guide which raises us from doing what we feel like doing, and toward doing that which is proper. That is a most essential ingredient in any relationship, and certainly in marriage. That our husband-wife relations are governed by what the Torah tells us is desirable goes a long way toward assuring that marital communication is on an exalted level.

It is too convenient to apply the notion of sacred service in marriage to the way husband and wife help each other. That help component is more directly associated with the third pillar, the practice of loving-kindness.

Sacred service here, and in marriage, refers to prayer. There are so many potential pitfalls that can intrude on marital harmony. We need to constantly pray to God that the marriage continues to thrive, that we never take the marriage for granted, nor the blessing of God that helps keep the marriage intact.

The practice of loving-kindness is precisely that – going out of the way to do nice things for one's life partner. Kindness begets kindness. The more kindness we do, the more kindness will ensue. And the more kindness, the stronger the relationship.

✤ MISHNAH 3 ✤

ג. אַנְטִיגְנוֹס אִישׁ סוֹכוֹ קִבֵּל מִשִּׁמְעוֹן הַצַּדִּיק. הוּא הָיָה אוֹמֵר: אַל תִּהְיוּ
כַעֲבָדִים הַמְשַׁמְּשִׁין אֶת הָרַב עַל מְנָת לְקַבֵּל פְּרָס, אֶלָּא הֱווּ כַעֲבָדִים
הַמְשַׁמְּשִׁין אֶת הָרַב שֶׁלֹּא עַל מְנָת לְקַבֵּל פְּרָס, וִיהִי מוֹרָא שָׁמַיִם עֲלֵיכֶם.

Antigones of Socho received the tradition from Shimon the Righteous. He
used to say: Be not like servants who serve their master for the sake of
receiving a reward; rather be like servants who serve their master not for the
sake of receiving a reward, and let the awe of Heaven be upon you.

One of the most important components of proper Torah-based
behavior is to acknowledge the good that has been done for you; to
say thank you with genuine appreciation.

What is important in general becomes even more important in
marriage, wherein the failure to say thank you properly is a breach
with more serious implications.

Whatever husband or wife do for the other needs to be acknowledged. All good deeds need to be re-enforced.

On the other hand, we open ourselves up to great hurt if we expect
this thank you "reward" as a matter of entitlement.

As wrong as it is to withhold gratitude, so is it wrong to expect,
even demand gratitude. Our service within marriage should be for its
own sake, without expectation of reward. Whatever comes should be
a bonus, rather than the basis for our actions.

⚜ MISHNAH 4 ⚜

ד. יוֹסֵי בֶּן יוֹעֶזֶר אִישׁ צְרֵדָה וְיוֹסֵי בֶּן יוֹחָנָן אִישׁ יְרוּשָׁלַיִם קִבְּלוּ מֵהֶם. יוֹסֵי בֶּן יוֹעֶזֶר אִישׁ צְרֵדָה אוֹמֵר: יְהִי בֵיתְךָ בֵּית וַעַד לַחֲכָמִים, וֶהֱוֵי מִתְאַבֵּק בַּעֲפַר רַגְלֵיהֶם, וֶהֱוֵי שׁוֹתֶה בַצָּמָא אֶת דִּבְרֵיהֶם.

Yose the son of Yoezer, of Tsereda, and Yose the son of Yohanan, of Yerushalayim, received the tradition from them [Shimon, Antigones, and the teachers who followed them]. Yose the son of Yoezer, of Tsereda, says; Let your house be a meeting place for the wise, cover yourself with the dust of their feet, and drink their words with thirst.

A couple who marry thereby take the first important step toward the ultimate goal, to build a Jewish home together permeated with the Jewish values articulated so clearly in Pirkay Avos and throughout the Torah and Talmud.

It is so easy to get caught up in the material concerns that go into making a home. Attention to those matters is not unimportant, but such attention needs to be placed into proper focus. Nothing is as important as the spiritual atmosphere of the home. If the Torah values are to be expressed, they need to be at home in the home.

What better way to achieve this than to make the home a *meeting place for the wise*. What better way to assure that the conversation of the wise becomes the basis for the home environment than to literally be so close to them, listening so attentively, that the dust of their feet covers you, and the words which they share are absorbed by you, the householder.

In this way, you will make of the marriage and the home created by the marriage a place where you share a common destiny as a couple, committed in tandem to promulgating the words of the sages, in a relationship that transcends mere mutual need gratification.

❧ MISHNAH 5 ❧

ה. יוֹסֵי בֶּן יוֹחָנָן אִישׁ יְרוּשָׁלַיִם אוֹמֵר: יְהִי בֵיתְךָ פָּתוּחַ לִרְוָחָה, וְיִהְיוּ
עֲנִיִּים בְּנֵי בֵיתֶךָ, וְאַל תַּרְבֶּה שִׂיחָה עִם הָאִשָּׁה. בְּאִשְׁתּוֹ אָמְרוּ, קַל וָחֹמֶר
בְּאֵשֶׁת חֲבֵרוֹ. מִכָּאן אָמְרוּ חֲכָמִים: כָּל הַמַּרְבֶּה שִׂיחָה עִם הָאִשָּׁה גּוֹרֵם
רָעָה לְעַצְמוֹ, וּבוֹטֵל מִדִּבְרֵי תוֹרָה, וְסוֹפוֹ יוֹרֵשׁ גֵּיהִנֹּם.

*Yose the son of Yohanan, of Yerushalayim, says: Let your house be opened
wide, let the poor be members of your household, and do not engage in excessive idle chatter with women. This was said with regard to one's wife; how
much more does it apply to a friend's wife. From this the sages derived that
one who engages in excessive idle chatter with women causes harm to himself
and desists from Torah study, and his end is that he will inherit Gehinnom.*

Kindness is one of the key ingredients for a house to be a Jewish
home. It is certainly vital that the conversation in the home be of a
sage quality, but the point of all this is missed if the home does not
put into actual practice the message of all the sage teaching. And the
practice begins with acts of kindness.

What could be a more tangible manifestation of this kindness
than the fact that the house is opened wide, that it is a house which
literally says – welcome, please come in. And what better proof that
the welcome is genuinely extended than that the poor actually feel
like members of the house; they feel they are at home.

However, all this kindness can come at a severe price. It is a price
too severe if the openness of the home comes at the expense of the
husband's relationship with his wife. This can occur if the husband
sees his wife as nothing more than a housekeeper who ensures that the
doors are always open, that the poor are properly fed, that everyone
is sufficiently entertained.

This demeaning attitude toward one's wife comes through in the
type of conversation one has with one's wife. Is it all about small
matters, mostly idle and insignificant chatter? Or is it a relationship
of abiding respect, wherein husband and wife deal with serious issues
together, and yes, do the husband and wife actually study Torah
together?

Kindness in the home is vital, but not when it is at the expense of a kindness-based relationship of respect between the spouses. Demeaning your wife, having a demeaning attitude to women in general, is harmful to the demeanor, whose attitude reflects an arrogance and false sense of superiority that undermines any Torah learning and leads to destructive, hellish consequences.

❧ MISHNAH 6 ❧

ו. יְהוֹשֻׁעַ בֶּן פְּרַחְיָה וְנִתַּאי הָאַרְבֵּלִי קִבְּלוּ מֵהֶם. יְהוֹשֻׁעַ בֶּן פְּרַחְיָה אוֹמֵר:
עֲשֵׂה לְךָ רַב, וּקְנֵה לְךָ חָבֵר, וֶהֱוֵי דָן אֶת כָּל הָאָדָם לְכַף זְכוּת.

Yehoshua the son of Perahya and Nittai of Arbel received the tradition from
them [Yose the son of Yoezer and Yose the son of Yohanan]. Yehoshua the
son of Perahya says: Make for yourself a teacher, acquire for yourself a
companion, and judge all individuals charitably.

What happens when you make for yourself a teacher is that you
thereby entrench, in a tangible way, the desire to learn, and to improve.
This means that you are ready and committed to be better today than
you were yesterday, and not as good as you will be tomorrow.

Applied to marriage, it suggests a readiness not to rest on laurels,
or be satisfied with the status quo. Instead, it affirms a resolve to make
what is hopefully an already good marriage into an even better union.
To be a student in the world of marriage, to continually strive to learn
new ways to improve the marriage, is the necessary and vital step to
help make that actually happen.

As much as we need teachers, we also need companions, to whom
and with whom we can share our innermost thoughts and concerns,
in full trust, and with a confidence that we will be understood and
responded to with complete dedication. Who better to fill that vital
role than the spouse, who is as one with you, and fully intertwined in
your present and future.

Ideal companionship flows within an atmosphere of trust and
mutual dedication. But at times in the developing relationship, there
can be lows, conflicts born of dispute or misunderstanding. We are
urged to give each other the benefit of the doubt, to impute good
motives and good intentions to the other; to judge the other charitably, on the side of merit, and to thereby assure that the disputes and
misunderstandings do not escalate into full-fledged feuds.

❧ MISHNAH 7 ❧

ז. נִתַּאי הָאַרְבֵּלִי אוֹמֵר: הַרְחֵק מִשָּׁכֵן רָע, וְאַל תִּתְחַבֵּר לָרָשָׁע, וְאַל תִּתְיָאֵשׁ מִן הַפֻּרְעָנוּת.

Nittai of Arbel says: Keep far away from a bad neighbor, do not consort with a wicked person, and do not despair of retribution.

This statement seems far removed from the marital sphere, yet there is an important message for the couple.

It is that they should choose their neighbors and their friends wisely. Marriage is more than a one-to-one relationship, though it is surely that.

For a marriage to flourish in all dimensions, a value-infused community is vital. The community enhances the couple with its concern, with its kindness, with its activities. A marriage does not exist in a vacuum.

At the same time, a marital couple enhanced by the community likewise strengthens that community.

Do not be fooled by what seems to be a flourishing neighborhood, but which is bereft of the ingredients needed to have an atmosphere of helpfulness. Go to the good, not to the fancy.

Choose solid people as friends, friends with solid values, not friends who are successful but whose values are questionable. They may seem to be on top of the world, but their success is fleeting and their day of reckoning will come.

❧ MISHNAH 8 ❧

ח. יְהוּדָה בֶּן טַבַּאי וְשִׁמְעוֹן בֶּן שָׁטַח קִבְּלוּ מֵהֶם. יְהוּדָה בֶּן טַבַּאי אוֹמֵר: אַל תַּעַשׂ עַצְמְךָ כְּעוֹרְכֵי הַדַּיָּנִין, וּכְשֶׁיִּהְיוּ בַּעֲלֵי הַדִּין עוֹמְדִים לְפָנֶיךָ יִהְיוּ בְּעֵינֶיךָ כִּרְשָׁעִים, וּכְשֶׁנִּפְטָרִים מִלְפָנֶיךָ יִהְיוּ בְעֵינֶיךָ כְּזַכָּאִין, כְּשֶׁקִּבְּלוּ עֲלֵיהֶם אֶת הַדִּין.

Yehuda the son of Tabbai and Shimon the son of Shetah received the tradition from them [Yehoshua the son of Perahya and Nittai of Arbel]. Yehuda the son of Tabbai says: In the office of judge do not act as counsel, and when the litigants stand before you consider them as guilty, but when they depart from you having accepted the judgment, consider them as innocent.

In life, we are often involved in making judgements, and not necessarily in a courtroom situation.

We may not realize it, but we are constantly assessing – what to wear, what to eat, what to do with free time, are just a few examples. Other judgements are not as benign. They involve other people, and our interaction with them.

We may look negatively on the actions of others, and even become deeply upset, specially if the action concerns one's spouse.

Bringing our concerns to the fore for discussion in a respectful manner will often be helpful, certainly more helpful than stewing on the inside.

Once the situation has been discussed, and matters clarified, including the possibility that one may have erred in their initial judgement, it is time to move on as if nothing happened.

✤ MISHNAH 9 ✤

ט. שִׁמְעוֹן בֶּן שָׁטַח אוֹמֵר: הֱוֵי מַרְבֶּה לַחֲקוֹר אֶת הָעֵדִים, וֶהֱוֵי זָהִיר בִּדְבָרֶיךָ,
שֶׁמָּא מִתּוֹכָם יִלְמְדוּ לְשַׁקֵּר.

Shimon the son of Shetah says: Examine the witnesses thoroughly, and be careful with your words, lest through them they learn to lie.

In trying to understand an issue that may arise between the couple, it is important to work the issue through in a careful and caring manner.

This means that the discussion should be carried out with patience, with care, with understanding.

To truly find out what is bothering your spouse, do not impose your thoughts, or put words in their mouth.

The spouse needs to feel free and comfortable to share thoughts and feelings in a pressure free, honesty evoking atmosphere.

Any discussion in the background of anger, or threats, is not likely to yield a positive result, an effective resolution.

❧ MISHNAH 10 ❧

י. שְׁמַעְיָה וְאַבְטַלְיוֹן קִבְּלוּ מֵהֶם. שְׁמַעְיָה אוֹמֵר: אֱהוֹב אֶת הַמְּלָאכָה וּשְׂנָא
אֶת הָרַבָּנוּת וְאַל תִּתְוַדַּע לָרָשׁוּת.

Shemaya and Avtalyon received the tradition from them [Yehuda the son of Tabbai and Shimon the son of Shetah]. Shemaya says: Love work, hate positions of lordship, and do not seek to become intimate with the ruling authorities.

If we add the word "marriage" to this directive, it yields the following understanding.

Love working on the marriage, constantly striving to make it better.

Approach marriage with the firm embrace of your spouse as a fully equal partner. In the humility of that approach, you will not impose or boss around. Instead, you will listen, learn, and react appropriately.

And avoid ingratiating yourself to others by sharing your troubles with them when there is no value to this unburdening except to curry favor.

To talk to others, in confidence, when they can possibly be helpful is understandable. To talk to others when there is no such possibility is unacceptable.

❧ MISHNAH 11 ❧

יא. אַבְטַלְיוֹן אוֹמֵר: חֲכָמִים, הִזָּהֲרוּ בְדִבְרֵיכֶם, שֶׁמָּא תָחוּבוּ חוֹבַת גָּלוּת
וְתִגְלוּ לִמְקוֹם מַיִם הָרָעִים, וְיִשְׁתּוּ הַתַּלְמִידִים הַבָּאִים אַחֲרֵיכֶם וְיָמוּתוּ,
וְנִמְצָא שֵׁם שָׁמַיִם מִתְחַלֵּל.

*Avtalyon says: Scholars – be careful with your words lest you incur the
penalty of exile, and will be exiled to a place of evil waters, and the disciples
who follow you will drink from them and die, and thus the name of Heaven
will be profaned.*

The message of Avtalyon is that when a person is in a position of trust,
there is an extra responsibility to be careful with one's words.

Teachers who are not precise in their teaching may cause unsus-
pecting students to misunderstand, misinterpret, and be misled into
serious error.

Marriage is a relationship of trust. The caution to be careful of what
one says to one's spouse is useful advice. A misunderstanding can
easily result from being less than careful with one's words, potentially
leading to a downward spiral in the relationship, into the exile of
loneliness and estrangement, and its unwelcome consequences.

❧ MISHNAH 12 ❧

יב. הִלֵּל וְשַׁמַּאי קִבְּלוּ מֵהֶם. הִלֵּל אוֹמֵר: הֱוֵי מִתַּלְמִידָיו שֶׁל אַהֲרֹן - אוֹהֵב
שָׁלוֹם וְרוֹדֵף שָׁלוֹם, אוֹהֵב אֶת הַבְּרִיּוֹת, וּמְקָרְבָן לַתּוֹרָה.

Hillel and Shammai received the tradition from them [Shemaya and Avtalyon]. Hillel says: Be of the disciples of Aharon – loving peace and pursuing peace, loving humankind and bringing them near to the Torah.

The great blessing that we associate with marriage is shalom bayit, peace in the home; or more precisely, tranquility of the home.

Shalom as peace, as the absence of any fighting, is good, but hardly enough. A marriage without fighting might survive, but is hardly fulfilling. A marriage defined by tranquility is one wherein there is an ease of communication, grounded in love and understanding.

The first step toward achieving this level of relationship is to appreciate its importance; to love peace and tranquility.

Once having apprehended its importance, the next step is to pursue it, by being understanding, by being patient, by being loving, by making the time for tranquility to unfold.

Studying together important Torah texts in an atmosphere of respect goes a long way toward entrenching tranquility as the permeating reality of the home.

❧ MISHNAH 13 ❧

יג. הוּא הָיָה אוֹמֵר: נְגַד שְׁמָא אֲבַד שְׁמֵהּ, וּדְלָא מוֹסִיף יָסֵף, וּדְלָא יַלִּיף קְטָלָא חַיָּב, וּדְאִשְׁתַּמֵּשׁ בְּתַגָּא חֲלָף.

He [Hillel] used to say: One who seeks a name loses one's name, one who does not increase knowledge decreases it, one who does not study deserves to die, and one who makes use of the crown will die.

This Mishnah addresses the matter of authenticity, of why we do what we do.

Life needs to be approached with humility. Humility includes not doing things for personal gain, because the more one's focus is on one's self, the less likely one is to develop into a worthy person.

Rather than seeking a name, a person within marriage should seek to enhance the other – one's marital partner. In humility, one should realize there is always more to learn; that thinking one knows everything is the way to choke off growth, to choke off life itself.

And to gloat over one's good deeds instead of seeing goodness as the natural way to be, is to head in a downward direction.

❧ MISHNAH 14 ☙

יד. הוּא הָיָה אוֹמֵר: אִם אֵין אֲנִי לִי, מִי לִי; וּכְשֶׁאֲנִי לְעַצְמִי, מָה אֲנִי; וְאִם
לֹא עַכְשָׁו, אֵימָתָי.

*He [Hillel] used to say: If I am not for myself, who is for me? When I am
for myself only, what am I? And if not now, when?*

This Mishnah comes so close to being a mantra for marriage.

One cannot enter marriage as a totally dependent being. It is unfair to expect of anyone else to look after all one's needs. One needs to be able to stand on one's own feet.

Having achieved a level of maturity, having addressed one's basic needs, the next step is to share, to go beyond one's self.

In marriage, founded on a measured confidence about one's own self, one extends to and embraces the other, immersing one's self in the other, naturally fulfilling the other and thereby reinforcing one's own self.

A marriage of mutual giving rather than mutual demanding is a marriage that is more likely to thrive.

A marriage in which "what can I do for you" is the main question, rather than "what can you, or must you do for me?" is a heavenly marriage of Hillel proportions.

In addition, if there is a sense of immediacy in one's commitment to one's spouse, a sense of "if not now, when," that further intensifies the mutual devotion defining the marriage.

❧ MISHNAH 15 ❧

טו. שַׁמַּאי אוֹמֵר: עֲשֵׂה תוֹרָתְךָ קֶבַע, אֱמוֹר מְעַט וַעֲשֵׂה הַרְבֵּה, וֶהֱוֵי מְקַבֵּל
אֶת כָּל הָאָדָם בְּסֵבֶר פָּנִים יָפוֹת.

*Shammai says: Make your Torah study a fixed duty, say little and do much,
and greet all people with a cheerful countenance.*

Obviously, this directive from Shammai is a general statement about
how to approach life.

Applied to marriage, it would translate into making the marriage,
and its success, a fixed duty that is not compromised. It is fixed, and
other less important matters gravitate around that fixed duty. Other
matters are flexible, duty to the marriage is not.

Then, with regard to marriage, it is always nice to try to make
things better, to resolve to improve. But words are not the key, deeds
are the key. Spend less time making resolutions and affirming desires,
and more time actually putting those nice ideas into practice. Deeds
make the difference, not the promise of doing deeds.

Finally, no matter the circumstance, always have a smile and a
cheer for your spouse. Even if you may not feel up to it, it is always
appropriate to lift up the spirits of your spouse by conveying a cheer,
a "I am always happy to see you" greeting.

These are all very welcome marriage enhancers.

✤ MISHNAH 16 ✤

טז. רַבָּן גַּמְלִיאֵל הָיָה אוֹמֵר: עֲשֵׂה לְךָ רַב, וְהִסְתַּלֵּק מִן הַסָּפֵק, וְאַל תַּרְבֶּה לְעַשֵּׂר אֲמָדוֹת.

Rabban Gamliel used to say: Provide for yourself a teacher and remove yourself from doubt, and do not give excessive tithe through guesswork.

Hardly anyone is so self-sufficient as to need no help from others, specially when it relates to situations wherein it is not clear what is the right approach to a problematic situation.

It helps to have a go-to person, a role model, who can give good, clear, objective advice on how to handle the situation.

Rather than just guesstimating what the right approach should be, taking counsel from someone who knows more, who has better experience, will be more helpful.

Handling complex situations in marriage with that approach may take more time, and energy, but it is well worth it.

Your taking the matter seriously rather than cavalierly will convey to your spouse how much you value the marriage, how caring and careful you are.

❧ MISHNAH 17 ❧

יז. שִׁמְעוֹן בְּנוֹ אוֹמֵר: כָּל יָמַי גָּדַלְתִּי בֵּין הַחֲכָמִים, וְלֹא מָצָאתִי לַגּוּף טוֹב מִשְּׁתִיקָה, וְלֹא הַמִּדְרָשׁ עִקָּר אֶלָּא הַמַּעֲשֶׂה, וְכָל הַמַּרְבֶּה דְבָרִים מֵבִיא חֵטְא.

Shimon his [Gamliel's] son says: All my days I have grown among the sages, and have found nothing better for the body than silence; study is not most important, rather doing, and one who proliferates words brings sin.

Rabban Shimon shares an observation from real life experience. Silence is not only good for the soul, it is good for the body.

Spending more time doing, and less time talking, keeps the entirety of one's persona active and engaged. It is important to know what to do, what to study. But the study must perforce lead to action.

In the view of Rabbenu Yonah, this speaks to a person's authenticity. One should not teach others what to do, and then not carry out the recommended approach.

Whoever is teaching others must already be a practitioner of what is being taught.

Whatever one desires in the behavior of one's spouse, one must already be doing that.

One whose actions are not consistent with one's teachings, or desires, embraces a hypocrisy that opens the door to cynicism and other negative repercussions.

❧ MISHNAH 18 ❧

יח. רַבָּן שִׁמְעוֹן בֶּן גַּמְלִיאֵל אוֹמֵר: עַל שְׁלֹשָׁה דְבָרִים הָעוֹלָם קַיָּם – עַל הַדִּין,
וְעַל הָאֱמֶת, וְעַל הַשָּׁלוֹם, שֶׁנֶּאֱמַר: אֱמֶת וּמִשְׁפַּט שָׁלוֹם שִׁפְטוּ בְּשַׁעֲרֵיכֶם.

*Rabban Shimon the son of Gamliel says: The world is preserved through
three things: justice, truth, and peace, as it is said – "administer truth and
the justice of peace in your gates." (ZEKHARYAH 8:16).*

Mishnah 2 dealt with the three pillars on which the world stands –
Torah, sacred service, and the *practice of loving kindness.* These are the
ultimate goals.

This concluding Mishnah deals with the requisites that are necessary in order to attain these goals, the ground rules of engagement.

Marriage is a small but self-contained world. The world of marriage
too must be based on justice, the fundamental legal obligations that
the spouses have to each other.

Truth refers to honesty, to respectful communication absent any
deception.

Justice and truth need to unfold in a peaceful, harmonious setting.
With the underpinning of these three fundamentals, the couple can
move forward to achieve a relationship that is firmly anchored and
able to continue growing in affection, trust, and reliability.

❧ EPILOGUE ❧

רַבִּי חֲנַנְיָא בֶּן עֲקַשְׁיָא אוֹמֵר: רָצָה הַקָּדוֹשׁ בָּרוּךְ הוּא לְזַכּוֹת אֶת יִשְׂרָאֵל, לְפִיכָךְ הִרְבָּה לָהֶם תּוֹרָה וּמִצְוֹת, שֶׁנֶּאֱמַר: יְהֹוָה חָפֵץ לְמַעַן צִדְקוֹ יַגְדִּיל תּוֹרָה וְיַאְדִּיר.

Rabbi Hananya the son of Akashya says: The Holy One, blessed is God, desired to make Israel worthy, and therefore gave them Torah and commandments in abundance, as it is said: "God desired, for the sake of Israel's righteousness, to magnify and glorify the Torah" (YESHAYAHU 42:21).

This closing observation is actually not a part of Pirkay Avos. Instead, it is an add-on when Pirkay Avos is studied from the first Shabbos after Pesah to the Shabbos before Rosh HaShanah.

As a closing observation, it addresses the perceived enormity of the obligations that confront us. Is not being loaded down with such a heavy weight of responsibilities almost a recipe for failure?

Here we are told that all these burdens are not intended to turn bad into good. The intent is to make the good better. We start off not as bad people, rather as good people capable of improving, even becoming worthy.

The abundance of obligations gives us a road map to becoming more worthy. True, no one will be able to completely fulfill all the obligations, including all the sage directives contained in this Talmudic tome.

But by having a proliferation of good things to actualize, we raise the bar of our aspirations, such that marriage, for example, can go from ordinary to extraordinary.

Because there is always room to improve, there is never room to be lax. Having a better relationship, making a good relationship better, is a never-ending endeavor.

Concluding each chapter with this encouragement reinforces the resolve to implement the exhortations just studied with even greater enthusiasm.

Chapter Two

א. רַבִּי אוֹמֵר: אֵיזוֹ הִיא דֶּרֶךְ יְשָׁרָה שֶׁיָּבוֹר לוֹ הָאָדָם, כָּל שֶׁהִיא תִּפְאֶרֶת לְעוֹשֶׂיהָ וְתִפְאֶרֶת לוֹ מִן הָאָדָם; וֶהֱוֵי זָהִיר בְּמִצְוָה קַלָּה כְּבַחֲמוּרָה, שֶׁאֵין אַתָּה יוֹדֵעַ מַתַּן שְׂכָרָן שֶׁל מִצְוֹת; וֶהֱוֵי מְחַשֵּׁב הֶפְסֵד מִצְוָה כְּנֶגֶד שְׂכָרָה, וּשְׂכַר עֲבֵרָה כְּנֶגֶד הֶפְסֵדָהּ. הִסְתַּכֵּל בִּשְׁלשָׁה דְבָרִים, וְאֵין אַתָּה בָא לִידֵי עֲבֵרָה – דַּע מַה לְמַעְלָה מִמְּךָ, עַיִן רוֹאָה וְאֹזֶן שׁוֹמַעַת, וְכָל מַעֲשֶׂיךָ בַּסֵּפֶר נִכְתָּבִים.

Rabbe [Yehuda haNasi] says: Which is the right path that a person should choose? That which is an honor to the one who does it and which also brings honor from humankind; be scrupulous with a light precept as with a weighty one, for you do not know the reward given for each precept; reckon the loss incurred in the performance of a commandment against its reward, and the gain obtained through committing a transgression against its loss. Concentrate on three things and you will not fall into the grip of sin – know what is above you: a seeing eye, a hearing ear, and all your deeds being recorded in the book.

In marriage, the way to choose is that which is honest to one's marital responsibility and which is appreciated by one's spouse.

The matters which you might consider minor are not necessarily thought of that way by your marital partner. Little things do matter, and make an impact. A little neglect might be perceived more seriously than it seems. A small gesture that might seem trivial might be huge in the eyes of your partner.

So, make sure not to downplay the importance of the little things. And be aware that all that one does, or says, is noticed, even if the reaction is not immediate.

✿ MISHNAH 2 ✿

ב. רַבָּן גַּמְלִיאֵל בְּנוֹ שֶׁל רַבִּי יְהוּדָה הַנָּשִׂיא אוֹמֵר: יָפֶה תַלְמוּד תּוֹרָה עִם
דֶּרֶךְ אֶרֶץ שֶׁיְּגִיעַת שְׁנֵיהֶם מַשְׁכַּחַת עָוֹן, וְכָל תּוֹרָה שֶׁאֵין עִמָּהּ מְלָאכָה
סוֹפָהּ בְּטֵלָה וְגוֹרֶרֶת עָוֹן. וְכָל הָעוֹסְקִים עִם הַצִּבּוּר יִהְיוּ עוֹסְקִים עִמָּהֶם
לְשֵׁם שָׁמַיִם, שֶׁזְּכוּת אֲבוֹתָם מְסַיְּעָתַם וְצִדְקָתָם עוֹמֶדֶת לָעַד, וְאַתֶּם, מַעֲלֶה
אֲנִי עֲלֵיכֶם שָׂכָר הַרְבֵּה כְּאִלּוּ עֲשִׂיתֶם.

*Rabban Gamliel, the son of Rabbe Yehuda haNasi, says: The study of Torah
combined with an occupation is an excellent thing, for the exertion demanded
by both together causes sin to be forgotten, while any Torah study without
work ultimately fails and causes sin. Let all who occupy themselves with the
community do so for the sake of Heaven, for the merit of their ancestors
sustains them and their righteousness endures forever. And as for you [says
God], I consider you worthy of great reward as if you had accomplished it.*

This Mishnah speaks eloquently about the balance between the
material and the spiritual.

In marriage, one dare not be oblivious to the immediate needs for
sustenance, and the importance of a life imbued with the values of
the Torah and the study thereof.

When the partners are together committed to a life of such bal-
anced purpose, they will stay on track and strengthen each other in
that common endeavor.

Marriage works best when the couple transcend each other toward
a higher purpose.

Whether or not they attain that purpose, the quest itself is worthy
in and of itself.

❧ MISHNAH 3 ❧

ג. הֱווּ זְהִירִין בָּרָשׁוּת, שֶׁאֵין מְקָרְבִין לוֹ לְאָדָם אֶלָּא לְצֹרֶךְ עַצְמָן. נִרְאִין
כְּאוֹהֲבִין בִּשְׁעַת הֲנָאָתָן, וְאֵין עוֹמְדִין לוֹ לְאָדָם בִּשְׁעַת דָּחֳקוֹ.

*Be cautious with the ruling authorities, for they befriend a person only for
their own needs. They appear as friends when it is to their advantage, but
they do not stand by the individual at the time of that person's distress.*

This Mishnah addresses a key element of relationships. There are
different types of relationships, and not only of the good variety.

There are those that seem good on the surface, but are more
alliances of common interests rather than unshakable friendships.

No matter how much one may want to be really good friends
with ruling authorities, the likelihood is that it is only a one-way
expression.

Ruling authorities rarely go beyond the superficial, and the immediate moment. What appears to be a friendship is more realistically
an alliance that will crumble as soon as the relationship offers no
advantage to the person in power.

The same is true of marriage. It can be a profound relationship.
But it can also be an alliance for personal gain under the guise of true
love.

The moment the veneer comes off, the relationship collapses. The
true nature of the relationship comes through most clearly in times
of distress, in times of challenge. True love brings out the best in the
worst of times.

❧ MISHNAH 4 ❧

ד. הוּא הָיָה אוֹמֵר: עֲשֵׂה רְצוֹנוֹ כִּרְצוֹנְךָ, כְּדֵי שֶׁיַּעֲשֶׂה רְצוֹנְךָ כִּרְצוֹנוֹ. בַּטֵּל
רְצוֹנְךָ מִפְּנֵי רְצוֹנוֹ, כְּדֵי שֶׁיְּבַטֵּל רְצוֹן אֲחֵרִים מִפְּנֵי רְצוֹנֶךָ.

*He [Rabban Gamliel] used to say: Do God's will as if it were your own
will, so that God may do your will as if it were God's will. Nullify your will
before God's will, so that God may nullify the will of others before your will.*

It is a well-known observation that when the marital couple are meritorious, the Divine presence dwells with them (Talmud, Sotah 17a).

In the magic of marriage at its best, each brings out the best in the other. Each one rushes to do what is best for the other, and sees it not as a bother; more like a privilege.

Without being asked, each one places their life partner ahead of their own self, nullifying their own will in favor of the will of their spouse, and doing for the spouse as if it were being done for one's own self.

Who makes the first move in that direction? It never works well when each one waits for the other. It works perfectly when each one makes the first move, without any expectations; just with the firm resolve that this is the right way to act.

Rabban Gamliel, in describing the ideal in our relationship with God, simultaneously describes the heavenly marriage relationship.

❧ MISHNAH 5 ❧

ה. הִלֵּל אוֹמֵר: אַל תִּפְרוֹשׁ מִן הַצִּבּוּר, וְאַל תַּאֲמִין בְּעַצְמְךָ עַד יוֹם מוֹתָךְ,
וְאַל תָּדִין אֶת חֲבֵרְךָ עַד שֶׁתַּגִּיעַ לִמְקוֹמוֹ, וְאַל תֹּאמַר דָּבָר שֶׁאִי אֶפְשָׁר
לִשְׁמֹעַ שֶׁסּוֹפוֹ לְהִשָּׁמַע, וְאַל תֹּאמַר לִכְשֶׁאֶפָּנֶה אֶשְׁנֶה, שֶׁמָּא לֹא תִפָּנֶה.

*Hillel says: Do not separate yourself from the community; do not be sure of
yourself until the day of your death; do not judge your fellow until you have
been in that person's position; do not say of a thing that it cannot possibly be
understood, for ultimately it will be understood; and do not say – "when I
have leisure I will study," for you may never have leisure.*

There is abundant marital advice in this Mishnah. Even though life at
home may be ideal, still it is best to see each marriage as a community
building block. Your spouse is your priority, but your community must
remain a focus of your concern; never separate from it.

Things may be going well at home, but never presume that is the
way it will always be. Keep at improving the relationship to the very
last moment, including the final parting.

Your spouse's actions and reactions may not measure up to your
expectations, but he or she is not you, and works within different
rational and emotional parameters. As close as you may be, you still
are not in your spouse's position, so do not judge.

If your spouse does not understand your behavior, try to explain
it. Do not think the other will never understand why you behaved as
you did. And in the patient process of explaining, you may even gain
some enlightenment about yourself.

Finally, never put off an issue between you till later when you have
time. For matters between you, be sure to make the time.

❧ MISHNAH 6 ❧

ו. הוּא הָיָה אוֹמֵר: אֵין בּוּר יְרֵא חֵטְא, וְלֹא עַם הָאָרֶץ חָסִיד, וְלֹא הַבַּישָׁן לָמֵד, וְלֹא הַקַּפְּדָן מְלַמֵּד, וְלֹא כָל הַמַּרְבֶּה בִסְחוֹרָה מַחְכִּים, וּבְמָקוֹם שֶׁאֵין אֲנָשִׁים, הִשְׁתַּדֵּל לִהְיוֹת אִישׁ.

He [Hillel] used to say: The empty person cannot be sin-fearing, the ignorant person cannot be pious, the diffident person cannot learn, the temperamental person cannot teach, and not everyone who is deeply involved in business becomes wise. And in a place where there are no people, strive to be a person.

Sin-fearing and piety are important in all spheres of life, including marriage. To avoid doing anything wrong, such as insulting one's spouse, and to focus on doing what is right and proper, what is pious, are critical to marriage.

There is always room to improve, room to learn more about one's spouse, their likes and dislikes, in order to improve the relationship.

Conveying all this in a calm, respectful manner is likewise critical. Making the time to listen and to learn, to spend less time at work and more time at home, also goes a long way toward marital fulfillment.

Finally, if it seems that your spouse is not eager or receptive to make things better, you should not see this as an excuse to do the same; instead it should be the motivation for you to be the person who leads the move to improve.

❧ MISHNAH 7 ❧

ז. אַף הוּא רָאָה גֻלְגֹּלֶת אַחַת שֶׁצָּפָה עַל פְּנֵי הַמָּיִם. אָמַר לָהּ: עַל דְּאַטֵּפְתְּ
אַטְפוּךְ, וְסוֹף מְטַיְּפַיִךְ יְטוּפוּן.

*Moreover, he [Hillel] saw a skull on the surface of the water. He said to it:
Because you drowned others, they drowned you, and ultimately, those who
drowned you will themselves be drowned.*

When there is no person to rise above the fray, when it is everyone
out for themselves, the end result can be quite violent.

But even in the absence of violence, there can still be serious and
unwelcome repercussions from being self-absorbed, uncaring, and
insensitive.

The down spiral from such a dynamic within marriage leads to
argument, counter argument, nastiness, and collapse.

There is a tendency to point the finger at the other as being the
one responsible for the relationship going sour, but it is hardly ever
a one-sided blame.

It usually takes two to spoil a union, and the implications usually
fall on both of them. No one escapes the tentacles of nastiness.

❧ MISHNAH 8 ❧

ח. הוּא הָיָה אוֹמֵר: מַרְבֶּה בָשָׂר מַרְבֶּה רִמָּה, מַרְבֶּה נְכָסִים מַרְבֶּה דְאָגָה, מַרְבֶּה נָשִׁים מַרְבֶּה כְשָׁפִים, מַרְבֶּה שְׁפָחוֹת מַרְבֶּה זִמָּה, מַרְבֶּה עֲבָדִים מַרְבֶּה גָזֵל. מַרְבֶּה תוֹרָה מַרְבֶּה חַיִּים, מַרְבֶּה יְשִׁיבָה מַרְבֶּה חָכְמָה, מַרְבֶּה עֵצָה מַרְבֶּה תְבוּנָה, מַרְבֶּה צְדָקָה מַרְבֶּה שָׁלוֹם. קָנָה שֵׁם טוֹב קָנָה לְעַצְמוֹ, קָנָה לוֹ דִּבְרֵי תוֹרָה קָנָה לוֹ חַיֵּי הָעוֹלָם הַבָּא.

He [Hillel] used to say: The more flesh, the more worms; the more possessions, the more worry; the more women, the more witchcraft; the more maidservants, the more lewdness; the more men-servants, the more robbery. The more Torah, the more life; the more schooling, the more wisdom; the more counsel, the more understanding; the more charity, the more peace. One who has acquired a good name has made an acquisition for the self; one who has acquired the words of Torah has acquired life in the world-to-come.

The essential message of Hillel is that material items, the tangibles, may seem more desirable, but after a point actually are detrimental to life.

On the other hand, as far as the intangibles are concerned, the value laden pursuits, more is better.

Gaining wisdom, seeking and enhancing wisdom, and implementing wise strategies to help those in need, are all uplifting and helpful.

A wise, charitable home in which the couple are devoted together not only to each other but to the world around them, creates a meaningful environment of caring wherein each is uplifted by the other.

It goes beyond merely having a good name. Implementing Torah values carries with it the spark of eternality, of enduring values that are forever.

❧ MISHNAH 9 ❧

ט. רַבָּן יוֹחָנָן בֶּן זַכַּאי קִבֵּל מֵהִלֵּל וּמִשַׁמַּאי. הוּא הָיָה אוֹמֵר: אִם לָמַדְתָּ
תוֹרָה הַרְבֵּה, אַל תַּחֲזִיק טוֹבָה לְעַצְמָךְ, כִּי לְכַךְ נוֹצָרְתָּ.

*Rabban Yohanan the son of Zakkai received [the tradition] from Hillel and
Shammai. He used to say: If you have learned much Torah do not ascribe
any merit to yourself, because this is the purpose for which you were formed.*

This is an interesting caution regarding living up to one's responsibilities in life.

There is a tendency to feel good at doing good. That is more a
natural reflex. And perfectly legitimate.

After all, it makes no sense to feel bad about doing good. There is
little chance of good generating more good if doing good generates
negative feelings.

But there is a subtle yet important difference between feeling good
and thinking of one's self as good.

The appropriate dynamic is to embrace the good, to feel good about
doing good, and thereby to feel energized to fulfill even more good.

In other words, doing good paves the way for more, in Torah study,
in marital life. Being a good spouse is a fundamental responsibility,
but not deserving of special accolades.

This does not mean that the beneficiary of one's goodness should
not be full of gratitude, and express that gratitude. It means that the
one who bestows the good should not be on the lookout for thanks.

❧ MISHNAH 10 ❧

י. חֲמִשָּׁה תַלְמִידִים הָיוּ לוֹ לְרַבָּן יוֹחָנָן בֶּן זַכַּאי, וְאֵלּוּ הֵן: רַבִּי אֱלִיעֶזֶר בֶּן הוֹרְקְנוֹס, רַבִּי יְהוֹשֻׁעַ בֶּן חֲנַנְיָא, רַבִּי יוֹסֵי הַכֹּהֵן, רַבִּי שִׁמְעוֹן בֶּן נְתַנְאֵל, וְרַבִּי אֶלְעָזָר בֶּן עֲרָךְ.

Rabban Yohanan the son of Zakkai had five disciples. They are: Rabbe Eliezer the son of Horkenos, Rabbe Yehoshua the son of Hananya, Rabbe Yose the Kohen, Rabbe Shimon the son of Netanel, and Rabbe Elazar the son of Arakh.

Rabban Yohanan the son of Zakkai had more than five students. Why are only these five mentioned here?

There is a famous statement attributed to Rabbe (Talmud, Makkos 10a), who edited the Mishnah, including Pirkay Avos, that he learned much from his teachers, more from his colleagues, but most from his students.

According to Midrash Shmuel on Pirkay Avos, the students enumerated here are the students from whom Rabban Yohanan learned, because each in his own way was so outstanding.

Marriage is itself so ennobling, so uplifting, when each of the partners is able to learn from the other, because each is full of virtues that are worth embracing.

❧ MISHNAH 11 ❧

יא. הוּא הָיָה מוֹנֶה שְׁבָחָם: רַבִּי אֱלִיעֶזֶר בֶּן הוֹרְקְנוֹס בּוֹר סוּד שֶׁאֵינוֹ
מְאַבֵּד טִפָּה, רַבִּי יְהוֹשֻׁעַ בֶּן חֲנַנְיָא אַשְׁרֵי יוֹלַדְתּוֹ, רַבִּי יוֹסֵי הַכֹּהֵן חָסִיד,
רַבִּי שִׁמְעוֹן בֶּן נְתַנְאֵל יְרֵא חֵטְא, וְרַבִּי אֶלְעָזָר בֶּן עֲרָךְ כְּמַעְיָן הַמִּתְגַּבֵּר.

*He [Rabban Yohanan] used to enumerate their merits: Rabbe Eliezer the son
of Horkenos is a plastered cistern that does not lose a drop; Rabbe Yehoshua
the son of Hananya, happy is she who bore him; Rabbe Yose the Kohen is a
pious man; Rabbe Shimon the son of Netanel is a sin-fearing man; and Rabbe
Elazar the son of Arakh is like a spring which continuously increases its flow.*

All the virtues of these sages are great virtues for marriage. *Not losing a
drop*, translated as having a good memory, works well in remembering
those things that are important to one's spouse.

Being attentive and thereby alert to what these are is necessary to
realize this virtue.

Being generally nice, the type of whom the mother would be proud,
helps with marital interaction.

Piety, making sure to fulfill one's obligations, and being *sin-fearing*,
extra careful not to do anything insensitive or hurtful, likewise makes
for a better marital union.

Finally, a dynamic *spring*, looking for more ways to do nice things,
is a most welcome marriage enhancer.

✤ MISHNAH 12 ✤

יב. . הוּא הָיָה אוֹמֵר: אִם יִהְיוּ כָל חַכְמֵי יִשְׂרָאֵל בְּכַף מֹאזְנַיִם, וֶאֱלִיעֶזֶר בֶּן
הוֹרְקְנוֹס בְּכַף שְׁנִיָה, מַכְרִיעַ אֶת כֻּלָּם. אַבָּא שָׁאוּל אוֹמֵר מִשְׁמוֹ: אִם יִהְיוּ
כָּל חַכְמֵי יִשְׂרָאֵל בְּכַף מֹאזְנַיִם וֶאֱלִיעֶזֶר בֶּן הוֹרְקְנוֹס אַף עִמָּהֶם, וְאֶלְעָזָר
בֶּן עֲרָךְ בְּכַף שְׁנִיָה, מַכְרִיעַ אֶת כֻּלָּם.

He [Rabban Yohanan] used to say: If all the sages of Israel were in one pan
of the balance scale and Eliezer the son of Horkenos in the other, he would
outweigh them all. Abba Shaul said in his [Rabban Yohanan's] name: If all
the sages of Israel were in one pan of the balance scale, and even Eliezer the
son of Horkenos with them, and Elazar the son of Arakh in the other, he
would outweigh them all.

Two views are suggested here regarding students. One is that retaining everything that is taught is the most important attribute.

The other is that a dynamic spring which is able to perceive the thrust of the Torah and apply it to new situations is the most vital attribute.

Both are of overriding importance. The argument is about which is more important – retaining the tradition in its entirety or being able to apply, and thereby extend the tradition from generation to generation.

Insofar as marriage is concerned, remembering everything that is of crucial importance to one's spouse, and acting accordingly, is a great manifestation of caring.

Likewise, expanding the ways one shows appreciation and affection to one's spouse gives the marriage such welcome energy.

Which is more important? Both.

❧ MISHNAH 13 ❧

יג. אָמַר לָהֶם: צְאוּ וּרְאוּ אֵיזוֹ הִיא דֶרֶךְ טוֹבָה שֶׁיִּדְבַּק בָּהּ הָאָדָם. רַבִּי
אֱלִיעֶזֶר אוֹמֵר: עַיִן טוֹבָה. רַבִּי יְהוֹשֻׁעַ אוֹמֵר: חָבֵר טוֹב. רַבִּי יוֹסֵי אוֹמֵר:
שָׁכֵן טוֹב. רַבִּי שִׁמְעוֹן אוֹמֵר: הָרוֹאֶה אֶת הַנּוֹלָד. רַבִּי אֶלְעָזָר אוֹמֵר: לֵב
טוֹב. אָמַר לָהֶם: רוֹאֶה אֲנִי אֶת דִּבְרֵי אֶלְעָזָר בֶּן עֲרָךְ מִדִּבְרֵיכֶם, שֶׁבִּכְלָל
דְּבָרָיו דִּבְרֵיכֶם.

*He [Rabban Yohanan] said to them [his disciples]: Go forth and see which
is the good way to which a person should cleave. Rabbe Eliezer says – a good
eye; Rabbe Yehoshua says – a good friend; Rabbe Yose says – a good neighbor;
Rabbe Shimon says – one who foresees that which will be; Rabbe Elazar
says – a good heart. He [Rabban Yohanan] said to them: I prefer the words
of Elazar the son of Arakh to yours, for your words are included in his words.*

All these are welcome ingredients in marriage. A good eye means
seeing all the good in one's partner, and acknowledging that in a
meaningful way.

Being a good friend speaks to the comfort level the spouses have
with each other, and the ease of their communication on matters
large and small.

Good neighborliness is manifested in respectfulness for borders.
That too is important in marriage. Closeness is important, as is respect
for the other's space.

Anticipating issues or circumstances that might come up, and
therefore being better able to deal with them, is also essential to the
marriage functioning well. These range from livelihood issues to family
issues to schooling issues, to name just a few.

In the end, entering into marriage with a good, caring, and sensitive
heart incorporates all these vital ingredients.

❧ MISHNAH 14 ❧

יד. אָמַר לָהֶם: צְאוּ וּרְאוּ אֵיזוֹ הִיא דֶּרֶךְ רָעָה שֶׁיִּתְרַחֵק מִמֶּנָּה הָאָדָם. רַבִּי
אֱלִיעֶזֶר אוֹמֵר: עַיִן רָעָה. רַבִּי יְהוֹשֻׁעַ אוֹמֵר: חָבֵר רָע. רַבִּי יוֹסֵי אוֹמֵר: שָׁכֵן
רָע. רַבִּי שִׁמְעוֹן אוֹמֵר: הַלֹּוֶה וְאֵינוֹ מְשַׁלֵּם. אֶחָד הַלֹּוֶה מִן הָאָדָם כְּלֹוֶה
מִן הַמָּקוֹם, שֶׁנֶּאֱמַר: לֹוֶה רָשָׁע וְלֹא יְשַׁלֵּם, וְצַדִּיק חוֹנֵן וְנוֹתֵן. רַבִּי אֶלְעָזָר
אוֹמֵר: לֵב רָע. אָמַר לָהֶם: רוֹאֶה אֲנִי אֶת דִּבְרֵי אֶלְעָזָר בֶּן עֲרָךְ מִדִּבְרֵיכֶם,
שֶׁבִּכְלַל דְּבָרָיו דִּבְרֵיכֶם.

*He [Rabban Yohanan] said to them [his disciples]: Go forth and see which is
the evil way from which a person should keep distant. Rabbe Eliezer says – a
bad eye; Rabbe Yehoshua says – a bad friend; Rabbe Yose says – a bad
neighbor; Rabbe Shimon says – one who borrows and does not repay. One
who borrows from a person is as one who borrows from the Omnipresent,
as it is said: "The wicked person borrows and never repays, but the righteous
person is gracious and gives" (TEHILLIM 37:21); Rabbe Elazar says – a bad
heart. He [Rabban Yohanan] said to them: I prefer the words of Elazar the
son of Arakh to yours, for your words are included in his words.*

This is not exactly the polar opposite of the previous Mishnah, but
close to it.

A bad eye means always seeing the bad, always being critical and
hardly ever seeing and saying nice things. This is the perfect way to
ruin a relationship.

Being a bad friend suggests not creating a comfort level so that the
couple can talk out issues with ease and assurance of abiding concern.
That destroys a most vital means of communication that solidifies the
marriage.

Bad neighborliness, not respecting the dignity and space that the
other needs, is another terrible intrusion on marital tranquility.

Borrowing with no intention to repay is a most glaring example
of not caring about consequence. As long as I have what I need, who
cares what happens to the one who loses out? Being out for one's self
without caring for the other distorts the marital bond.

And of course, the bad heart incorporates all the horrible traits that can destroy any relationship, and certainly the marriage relationship, predicated as it is on good-heartedness, on caring for each other, on looking out for each other.

❧ MISHNAH 15 ❧

טו. הֵם אָמְרוּ שְׁלֹשָׁה דְבָרִים. רַבִּי אֱלִיעֶזֶר אוֹמֵר: יְהִי כְבוֹד חֲבֵרְךָ חָבִיב עָלֶיךָ כְּשֶׁלָּךְ, וְאַל תְּהִי נוֹחַ לִכְעוֹס, וְשׁוּב יוֹם אֶחָד לִפְנֵי מִיתָתָךְ. וֶהֱוֵי מִתְחַמֵּם כְּנֶגֶד אוּרָן שֶׁל חֲכָמִים, וֶהֱוֵי זָהִיר בְּגַחֲלָתָן שֶׁלֹּא תִכָּוֶה, שֶׁנְּשִׁיכָתָן נְשִׁיכַת שׁוּעָל, וַעֲקִיצָתָן עֲקִיצַת עַקְרָב, וּלְחִישָׁתָן לְחִישַׁת שָׂרָף, וְכָל דִּבְרֵיהֶם כְּגַחֲלֵי אֵשׁ.

They [the disciples of Rabban Yohanan] each stressed three things. Rabbe Eliezer says: Let your friend's honor be as dear to you as your own, do not be easily provoked to anger, and repent one day before your death. Be warmed by the fire of the sages but beware of their glowing coals lest you be burned, for their bite is the bite of a fox, their sting is the sting of a scorpion, their hiss is the hiss of a serpent, and all their words are like coals of fire.

Rabbe Eliezer, who recommends having a good eye as the overarching value, urges that we see others as worthy of being treated with respect.

Treating one's spouse with respect, verily seeing the importance of extending such respect as being on par with one's own being respected, is a good way to articulate the notion that one's spouse is literally like one's own corpus (see for example, Talmud, Kesubos 66a; Menahos 93b).

With such an attitude, one is as unlikely to become angry at one's spouse as one would be to getting angry at one's self.

And, following the understanding of the Talmud that repenting one day before one's death means that one should always be repenting since we never know which day is the last day (Talmud Shabbos, 153a), it means that we should always strive to be better.

Good today, better than yesterday, but not as good as tomorrow. The striving to be better is serious business, with profound consequences. Depending on how one approaches this endeavor, the relationship can either be warmed or singed.

❧ MISHNAH 16 ❧

טז. רַבִּי יְהוֹשֻׁעַ אוֹמֵר: עַיִן הָרָע, וְיֵצֶר הָרָע, וְשִׂנְאַת הַבְּרִיּוֹת, מוֹצִיאִין אֶת הָאָדָם מִן הָעוֹלָם.

Rabbe Yehoshua says: A bad eye, bad passion, and hatred of one's fellow drive a person out of the world.

Rabbe Yehoshua, who extols the virtue of being a good friend, here expounds on toxic behavior to be avoided at all costs. It destroys a person, and needless to say, destroys relationships.

Looking negatively at one's spouse, begrudging their success and well-being; i.e., having a bad eye, is obviously destructive.

A bad passion – when instead of engaging in a mutuality of giving, ones uses the other to fulfill one's lustful desires, such that the partner feels used, even abused, leading almost inevitably to the hatred of the other because of that despicable conduct – destroys the marriage.

The bad eye sees the other as a vehicle to engage one's narcissistic pursuits, the worst form of depersonalization. It is pure marital poison.

✤ MISHNAH 17 ✤

יז. רַבִּי יוֹסֵי אוֹמֵר: יְהִי מָמוֹן חֲבֵרְךָ חָבִיב עָלֶיךָ כְּשֶׁלָּךְ, וְהַתְקֵן עַצְמְךָ לִלְמוֹד תּוֹרָה שֶׁאֵינָהּ יְרֻשָּׁה לָךְ, וְכָל מַעֲשֶׂיךָ יִהְיוּ לְשֵׁם שָׁמָיִם.

Rabbe Yose says: Let your friend's possessions be as dear to you as your own, ready yourself for the study of Torah as it does not come to you through inheritance, and let all your actions be for the sake of Heaven.

Rabbe Yose, the man of piety, introduces us to the full extent of piety.

Respecting what belongs to others as if it were yours goes a long way in marriage. In marriage, valuing what your spouse values is a profound expression of sensitivity and respect.

And continuing to study the Torah, the teaching of marriage, even if you come from a respecting family that lived marriage properly, is likewise an act of piety. This is because the pious truly believe that you can always improve, that being good is not good enough; there is always room for better.

Ultimately, the obligation to one's spouse derives from the Godly sanctity of marriage, and of each person. Life is holy, each person is holy, the marriage is holy.

Through piously adhering to these values, the marriage is commensurately sanctified and ennobled.

✤ MISHNAH 18 ✤

יח. רַבִּי שִׁמְעוֹן אוֹמֵר: הֱוֵי זָהִיר בִּקְרִיאַת שְׁמַע וּבִתְפִלָּה. וּכְשֶׁאַתָּה
מִתְפַּלֵּל, אַל תַּעַשׂ תְּפִלָּתְךָ קֶבַע, אֶלָּא רַחֲמִים וְתַחֲנוּנִים לִפְנֵי הַמָּקוֹם,
שֶׁנֶּאֱמַר: כִּי חַנּוּן וְרַחוּם הוּא, אֶרֶךְ אַפַּיִם וְרַב חֶסֶד, וְנִחָם עַל הָרָעָה. וְאַל
תְּהִי רָשָׁע בִּפְנֵי עַצְמֶךָ.

Rabbe Shimon says: Be careful in the reading of the Shema and in prayer,
and when you pray, do not make your prayer a mechanical routine but an
appeal for mercy and graciousness before the Omnipresent, as it is said: "for
God is gracious and merciful, slow to anger and abounding in loving-kindness,
and relenting of the evil" (YOEL 2:13); and do not consider yourself wicked.

Rabbe Shimon, the sin-fearing man, stresses the importance of declaring abiding faith in God and approaching supplication to God with genuine sincerity.

The fidelity to God has its counterpart in marriage, wherein for each of the partners, there is no other aside from the real other, one's spouse.

Marital obligations are never to be treated lightly, and there are times when either of the partners falls short, is neglectful, or less than responsible.

The proper corrective is to admit one's failing, and to genuinely seek the spouse's forgiveness. That "prayer," that beseeching, must be sincere and heartfelt.

Additionally, failing to measure up should not translate into believing that one is wicked, incapable of doing better. That can easily morph into a self-fulfilling prophecy.

The sincere regret, the genuine entreaty, is ample evidence of one's inherent noble character.

❧ MISHNAH 19 ❧

יט. רַבִּי אֶלְעָזָר אוֹמֵר: הֱוֵי שָׁקוּד לִלְמוֹד תּוֹרָה, וְדַע מַה שֶׁתָּשִׁיב לְאֶפִּיקוֹרוֹס, וְדַע לִפְנֵי מִי אַתָּה עָמֵל, וּמִי הוּא בַּעַל מְלַאכְתֶּךָ שֶׁיְשַׁלֶם לְךָ שְׂכַר פְּעֻלָתֶךָ.

Rabbe Elazar says: Be diligent to study Torah, and know what to respond to a heretic; know before Whom you toil and Who your Employer is who will pay you the reward of your labor.

Rabbe Elazar, the proponent of having a good heart, is here suggesting that part of having a good heart is being prepared, knowing what to do; to have your heart in it.

To know what to do, one needs to know. To know, one needs to be diligent in the study of Torah.

To know what to do in marriage, one needs to diligently prepare, to be clear in one's duties, so clear as to be able to easily fend off scoffers who may question your dedication and selflessness.

Inherent in the responsibility to one's spouse is responsibility to God, the Ultimate Employer.

❧ MISHNAH 20 ❧

כ. רַבִּי טַרְפּוֹן אוֹמֵר: הַיּוֹם קָצֵר, וְהַמְּלָאכָה מְרֻבָּה, וְהַפּוֹעֲלִים עֲצֵלִים, וְהַשָּׂכָר הַרְבֵּה, וּבַעַל הַבַּיִת דּוֹחֵק.

Rabbe Tarfon says: The day is short, the task is great, the workers are lazy, the reward is great, and the Master of the house is insistent.

The task in marriage is to build a relationship of trust and love, based on a shared commitment to fulfill the Torah together.

Each act of caring, each act of mutual respect, each affirmation of love, is a building block toward that task.

The reward of realizing this noble goal is self-evident, but as humans we can sometimes put things off, and delay in responding, with the argument that there is so much time left to build the relationship.

We are here being told that we do not know how much time we have, and that every opportunity squandered is an opportunity lost that cannot be easily recovered.

Because of the enormity of the task, the day is by definition short. Every opportunity is therefore by definition an opportunity that should be embraced. The Master of the house insists on it, for our own good.

✤ MISHNAH 21 ✤

כא. הוּא הָיָה אוֹמֵר: לֹא עָלֶיךָ הַמְּלָאכָה לִגְמוֹר, וְלֹא אַתָּה בֶן חוֹרִין לְהִבָּטֵל מִמֶּנָה. אִם לָמַדְתָּ תוֹרָה הַרְבֵּה, נוֹתְנִין לְךָ שָׂכָר הַרְבֵּה, וְנֶאֱמָן הוּא בַּעַל מְלַאכְתֶּךָ שֶׁיְשַׁלֶּם לְךָ שְׂכַר פְּעֻלָתֶךָ. וְדַע שֶׁמַּתַּן שְׂכָרָן שֶׁל צַדִּיקִים לֶעָתִיד לָבֹא.

He [Rabbe Tarfon] used to say: It is not up to you to complete the task, but you are not free to desist from it. If you have studied much Torah, abundant reward will be given to you, and your Employer is faithful to pay you the reward of your work. But know that the payment of reward to the righteous is in the time to come.

Applied to marriage, no matter how much we strive to do our best in the marriage, there is always more to actualize.

Today's kind words and deeds are not an excuse for being lackadaisical tomorrow. We cannot complete the task, the task of attaining a perfect relationship. That is impossible.

But we can, and should strive toward perfection each day, fully aware that the goal is elusive, literally unreachable.

There is no room for complacency, because there is always room for improvement.

And the ultimate reward of this continuous striving is, by definition, other worldly.

Chapter Three

א. עֲקַבְיָא בֶּן מַהֲלַלְאֵל אוֹמֵר: הִסְתַּכֵּל בִּשְׁלֹשָׁה דְבָרִים, וְאֵין אַתָּה בָא לִידֵי עֲבֵרָה. דַּע מֵאַיִן בָּאתָ, וּלְאָן אַתָּה הוֹלֵךְ, וְלִפְנֵי מִי אַתָּה עָתִיד לִתֵּן דִּין וְחֶשְׁבּוֹן. מֵאַיִן בָּאתָ - מִטִּפָּה סְרוּחָה. וּלְאָן אַתָּה הוֹלֵךְ - לִמְקוֹם עָפָר רִמָּה וְתוֹלֵעָה. וְלִפְנֵי מִי אַתָּה עָתִיד לִתֵּן דִּין וְחֶשְׁבּוֹן - לִפְנֵי מֶלֶךְ מַלְכֵי הַמְּלָכִים, הַקָּדוֹשׁ בָּרוּךְ הוּא.

Akavya the son of Mahalalel says: Concentrate on three matters and you will not fall into the grip of sin. Know from where you came, where you are going, and before Whom you will have to give account and reckoning. From where you came – from a putrid drop. Where you are going – to a place of dust, worms, and maggots. And before Whom you will have to give account and reckoning – before the Supreme Ruler of rulers, the Holy One, blessed is God.

Being singularly aware of this exhortation is a wonderful hedge to arrogance, and a continual reminder to be careful in everything we do.

The interactions with our spouse may seem like private matters, but they remain matters of record, recorded matters for which we will need to answer.

Haughtiness is never acceptable, and even more so is it contemptible in marriage, wherein such behavioral attitude can cause so much pain and anguish.

Knowing our humble beginning and equally humble destination, and the exacting accountability that awaits us, should keep us from deviating off the track of caring and responsibleness.

❧ MISHNAH 2 ❧

ב. רַבִּי חֲנִינָא סְגַן הַכֹּהֲנִים אוֹמֵר: הֱוֵי מִתְפַּלֵּל בִּשְׁלוֹמָהּ שֶׁל מַלְכוּת,
שֶׁאִלְמָלֵא מוֹרָאָהּ אִישׁ אֶת רֵעֵהוּ חַיִּים בְּלָעוֹ.

*Rabbe Hanina, the deputy high priest, says: Pray for the welfare of the
government, for were it not for the fear thereof, people would swallow each
other alive.*

People who live in peace are peace loving. A couple who live in
harmony reap the rewards of a blessed life.

But we do not live in self-contained bubbles. As important as it
is to generate harmony within the home, that harmony can prosper
only if the general environment is peaceful.

Those who value peace in the home must by definition value peace
everywhere.

One very concrete way of manifesting this is by praying that peace
reigns all around, and that everyone will be able to reap the benefits
of that peace.

A couple who are blessed should together pray that these blessings
are enjoyed by the multitude. Everyone gains from such prayers.

❧ MISHNAH 3 ❧

ג. רַבִּי חֲנַנְיָא בֶּן תְּרַדְיוֹן אוֹמֵר: שְׁנַיִם שֶׁיּוֹשְׁבִין וְאֵין בֵּינֵיהֶם דִּבְרֵי תוֹרָה,
הֲרֵי זֶה מוֹשַׁב לֵצִים, שֶׁנֶּאֱמַר: וּבְמוֹשַׁב לֵצִים לֹא יָשָׁב. אֲבָל שְׁנַיִם שֶׁיּוֹשְׁבִין
וְיֵשׁ בֵּינֵיהֶם דִּבְרֵי תוֹרָה שְׁכִינָה שְׁרוּיָה בֵינֵיהֶם, שֶׁנֶּאֱמַר: אָז נִדְבְּרוּ יִרְאֵי יְיָ
אִישׁ אֶל רֵעֵהוּ, וַיַּקְשֵׁב יְיָ וַיִּשְׁמָע וַיִּכָּתֵב סֵפֶר זִכָּרוֹן לְפָנָיו לְיִרְאֵי יְיָ וּלְחֹשְׁבֵי
שְׁמוֹ. אֵין לִי אֶלָּא שְׁנַיִם, מִנַּיִן אֲפִילוּ אֶחָד שֶׁיּוֹשֵׁב וְעוֹסֵק בַּתּוֹרָה שֶׁהַקָּדוֹשׁ
בָּרוּךְ הוּא קוֹבֵעַ לוֹ שָׂכָר, שֶׁנֶּאֱמַר: יֵשֵׁב בָּדָד וְיִדֹּם כִּי נָטַל עָלָיו.

Rabbe Hananya the son of Teradyon says: Two who sit together and no words of Torah are exchanged between them, this constitutes a company of scorners, as it is said – "and never sat in the company of scorners…" (TEHILLIM 1:1). *But two who sit together and words of Torah are exchanged between them, the Divine Presence abides with them, as it is said – "Then they who were filled with the awe of God spoke with one another, and God took note and heard, and a book of remembrance was written before God for those who are in awe of God and dwell upon God's name"* (MALAKHI 3:16). *This only proves the case of two; from where can it be derived that even one who sits and is occupied with Torah, the Holy One, blessed is God, establishes recompense for that person? Because it is said – "Let him sit alone, and be at rest, for he has received that which was meant for him"* (AYKHAH 3:38).

Rabbe Hananya condemns the coming together of people who engage in conversation totally devoid of Torah.

Torah is a broad term that incorporates learning and action, purpose and meaning. There is room for light conversation, but getting together and having nothing but light conversation is a waste.

A married couple are urged to include meaning, purpose, and study in their conversation.

And it all begins with each on their own being oriented in that direction, so that when coming together, such type of conversation flows naturally.

❧ MISHNAH 4 ❧

ד. רַבִּי שִׁמְעוֹן אוֹמֵר: שְׁלֹשָׁה שֶׁאָכְלוּ עַל שֻׁלְחָן אֶחָד, וְלֹא אָמְרוּ עָלָיו
דִּבְרֵי תוֹרָה, כְּאִלּוּ אָכְלוּ מִזִּבְחֵי מֵתִים, שֶׁנֶּאֱמַר: כִּי כָּל שֻׁלְחָנוֹת מָלְאוּ
קִיא צוֹאָה בְּלִי מָקוֹם. אֲבָל שְׁלֹשָׁה שֶׁאָכְלוּ עַל שֻׁלְחָן אֶחָד וְאָמְרוּ עָלָיו
דִּבְרֵי תוֹרָה, כְּאִלּוּ אָכְלוּ מִשֻּׁלְחָנוֹ שֶׁל מָקוֹם, שֶׁנֶּאֱמַר: וַיְדַבֵּר אֵלַי, זֶה
הַשֻּׁלְחָן אֲשֶׁר לִפְנֵי יְיָ.

*Rabbe Shimon says: Three who have eaten at a table and have spoken
there no words of Torah, it is as if they had eaten from offerings to the
dead, as it is said – "For all their tables are full of vomit and filth with no
space" (YESHAYAHU 28:8). But three who have eaten at a table and have
spoken there words of Torah, it is as if they had eaten at the table of the
Omnipresent, as it is said: "and he said to me: this is the table that is before
the Lord" (YEHEZKEL 41:22).*

A married couple is two; the third, the fourth, are likely all those who
have joined for the meal.

A couple who are happy together, who respect and admire each
other, will likely transmit, in quiet dignity, the beauty of marital
togetherness.

In so doing, they will have transmitted the Torah of marriage by
profound example. Their guests will have eaten at God's table.

❧ MISHNAH 5 ❧

ה. רַבִּי חֲנִינָא בֶּן חֲכִינַאי אוֹמֵר: הַנֵּעוֹר בַּלַּיְלָה, וְהַמְהַלֵּךְ בַּדֶּרֶךְ יְחִידִי, וּמְפַנֶּה לִבּוֹ לְבַטָּלָה, הֲרֵי זֶה מִתְחַיֵּב בְּנַפְשׁוֹ.

Rabbe Hanina the son of Hakhinai says: One who keeps awake at night, or one who goes on the way alone, and makes room in the heart for idleness, forfeits one's soul.

In the view of Rabbenu Yonah, these two times, awake at night and alone on the way, are golden opportunities when one is undisturbed and can contemplate significant thoughts.

These are occasions when one can look at life, and at how one can improve.

Included in this room for improvement is how to make one's marriage better. Being better is a limitless goal. Often, there is little time to reflect, but when the time is available, it is sinful to squander it.

❧ MISHNAH 6 ❧

ו. רַבִּי נְחוּנְיָא בֶּן הַקָּנָה אוֹמֵר: כָּל הַמְקַבֵּל עָלָיו עוֹל תּוֹרָה, מַעֲבִירִין מִמֶּנּוּ
עוֹל מַלְכוּת וְעוֹל דֶּרֶךְ אֶרֶץ; וְכָל הַפּוֹרֵק מִמֶּנּוּ עוֹל תּוֹרָה, נוֹתְנִין עָלָיו עוֹל
מַלְכוּת וְעוֹל דֶּרֶךְ אֶרֶץ.

*Rabbe Nehunya the son of Hakana says: Whoever accepts upon one's self the
yoke of the Torah, the yoke of worldly occupation will be removed from that
person. But whoever casts from the self the yoke of Torah, the yoke of the
kingdom and the yoke of a worldly occupation are placed upon that person.*

For some people, the ability to live a stress-free life seems to be a most
desirable goal. What could be better than to have no worries.

But that is not the way life works. To be stress free is to be dead.
The choice before us is not stress vs. no stress. Rather, it is which
stress we choose.

If the focus is on the Torah in its entirety, the study and the fulfillment thereof, on living a meaningful Torah imbued life, everything
else folds nicely into that laudable desire.

Whether or not we are wealthy becomes secondary to whether we
are making a difference through our kindness and caring.

Thrusting off any desire to be helpful and responsive does not
relieve us of stress. It only makes room for other, less meaningful
stressors, such as pursuing material gain.

Striving to live up to the Torah ideal in marriage creates a centrality
of purpose that is welcome and fulfilling.

✤ MISHNAH 7 ✤

ז. רַבִּי חֲלַפְתָּא בֶּן דּוֹסָא אִישׁ כְּפַר חֲנַנְיָא אוֹמֵר: עֲשָׂרָה שֶׁיּוֹשְׁבִין וְעוֹסְקִין
בַּתּוֹרָה שְׁכִינָה שְׁרוּיָה בֵּינֵיהֶם, שֶׁנֶּאֱמַר: אֱלֹהִים נִצָּב בַּעֲדַת אֵל. וּמִנַּיִן אֲפִילוּ
חֲמִשָּׁה, שֶׁנֶּאֱמַר: וַאֲגֻדָּתוֹ עַל אֶרֶץ יְסָדָהּ. וּמִנַּיִן אֲפִילוּ שְׁלֹשָׁה, שֶׁנֶּאֱמַר:
בְּקֶרֶב אֱלֹהִים יִשְׁפֹּט. וּמִנַּיִן אֲפִילוּ שְׁנַיִם, שֶׁנֶּאֱמַר: אָז נִדְבְּרוּ יִרְאֵי יְיָ אִישׁ
אֶל רֵעֵהוּ, וַיַּקְשֵׁב יְיָ וַיִּשְׁמָע. וּמִנַּיִן אֲפִילוּ אֶחָד, שֶׁנֶּאֱמַר: בְּכָל הַמָּקוֹם אֲשֶׁר
אַזְכִּיר אֶת שְׁמִי, אָבֹא אֵלֶיךָ וּבֵרַכְתִּיךָ.

*Rabbe Halafta the son of Dosa of the village of Hananya says: Ten who
sit and occupy themselves with the Torah, the Divine Presence abides with
them, as it is said – "... God stands in the congregation of the Almighty..."*
(TEHILLIM 82:1). *And from where can it be derived that this applies in the
case of five? As it is said – "... God has founded God's band upon earth..."*
(AMOS 9:6). *And from where can it be derived that this applies even in the
case of three? As it is said – "in the midst of judges, God judges"* (TEHILLIM
82:1). *And from where can it be derived that this applies even in the case of
two? As it is said – "Then they who were in awe of God spoke to each other
and God listened and heard..."* (MALAKHI 3:16). *And from where can it
be derived that this applies even in the case of one? As it is said – "in every
place where I cause My Name to be remembered I will come and bless you"*
(SHEMOT 20:21).

Any gathering which has a Torah focus is praiseworthy. Torah in its
larger sense refers to more than merely studying the Torah. It refers
to implementing the Torah.

Implementation takes many forms, including gathering to set up
schools or prayer houses, agencies to feed the poor, caring for the
not well, or looking after the departed, among other noteworthy
endeavors.

Two who gather together in marriage, and resolve to not only care
for each other, but to also, in tandem, employ their collective strengths
to help others, to help build community, either through having an
open home and/or supporting communal institutions, will be blessed
with God's presence in their sacred, selfless aspirations.

It all starts with every individual on their own being oriented in this direction, such that the coming together in marriage goes beyond mutual self-fulfillment, and into the self-transcending dimension of building community.

❧ MISHNAH 8 ❧

ח. רַבִּי אֶלְעָזָר אִישׁ בַּרְתּוֹתָא אוֹמֵר: תֶּן לוֹ מִשֶּׁלּוֹ, שָׁאַתָּה וְשֶׁלְךָ שֶׁלּוֹ. וְכֵן בְּדָוִד הוּא אוֹמֵר: כִּי מִמְּךָ הַכֹּל וּמִיָּדְךָ נָתַנּוּ לָךְ.

Rabbe Eliezer of Bartosa says: Give God from what is God's, because you and all that you have are God's. And thus is it said of David – "for all things come from You and from Your own we have given to You" (I DIVRAY HAYAMIM 29:14).

What we have, whether it be each other, our time, or our material possessions, they are all gifts of God.

We are the trustees of these gifts, literally entrusted to put them all to exalted use.

Therefore, being nice, doing nice things, should not be seen as a sacrifice, as something that we are stuck having to do.

We are simply giving to God from what God gave to us. With such an attitude, we will not only give more, but we will be happy and grateful for the opportunity to give, to share.

This applies in significant measure to the time, the attention, and the love bestowed upon one's spouse.

❧ MISHNAH 9 ❧

ט. רַבִּי יַעֲקֹב אוֹמֵר: הַמְהַלֵּךְ בַּדֶּרֶךְ וְשׁוֹנֶה, וּמַפְסִיק מִמִּשְׁנָתוֹ וְאוֹמֵר – מַה נָּאֶה אִילָן זֶה, מַה נָּאֶה נִיר זֶה, מַעֲלֶה עָלָיו הַכָּתוּב כְּאִלּוּ מִתְחַיֵּב בְּנַפְשׁוֹ.

Rabbe Yaakov says: One who is walking by the way in study and interrupts the study to exclaim – "how beautiful is this tree!" "how beautiful is this field!" is regarded by Scripture as having forfeited one's soul.

There is nothing wrong, and everything right, with admiring nature, with expressing how wondrous is God's world.

And of course, studying God's Torah is a most eloquent affirmation of the essentiality of God's word.

There is room for both expressions. But there is a world of difference between God's word and God's work.

Rabbe Yaakov insists that we be sure to have our priorities in order. God's work is worthy of our praise, God's word demands our attention and careful study.

We dare not interrupt the study of God's word, even if it is to admire God's work. We should not interrupt a matter of utmost importance for a matter of lesser importance.

The lesson for marriage is evident. Attentiveness to one's spouse is of such importance that we give it our full attention, and not allow matters of lesser importance to interrupt that attentiveness.

❧ MISHNAH 10 ❧

י. רַבִּי דּוֹסְתָּאִי בְּרַבִּי יַנַּאי מִשּׁוּם רַבִּי מֵאִיר אוֹמֵר: כָּל הַשּׁוֹכֵחַ דָּבָר אֶחָד
מִמִּשְׁנָתוֹ, מַעֲלֶה עָלָיו הַכָּתוּב כְּאִלּוּ מִתְחַיֵּב בְּנַפְשׁוֹ, שֶׁנֶּאֱמַר: רַק הִשָּׁמֶר
לְךָ וּשְׁמֹר נַפְשְׁךָ מְאֹד פֶּן תִּשְׁכַּח אֶת הַדְּבָרִים אֲשֶׁר רָאוּ עֵינֶיךָ. יָכוֹל אֲפִילוּ
תָּקְפָה עָלָיו מִשְׁנָתוֹ, תַּלְמוּד לוֹמַר: וּפֶן יָסוּרוּ מִלְּבָבְךָ כֹּל יְמֵי חַיֶּיךָ - הָא
אֵינוֹ מִתְחַיֵּב בְּנַפְשׁוֹ עַד שֶׁיֵּשֵׁב וִיסִירֵם מִלִּבּוֹ.

Rabbe Dostai the son of Yannai said in the name of Rabbe Meir: Whoever forgets one word of study is regarded by Scripture as having forfeited one's soul, as it is said – "Only take heed of yourself, and diligently guard your soul, lest you forget the things that your eyes have seen . . ." (DEVARIM 4:9). Lest it be presumed that this applies even when study was too difficult, for this the Torah adds – "and lest they depart from your heart all the days of your life . . ." (DEVARIM 4:9). That means one does not forfeit one's soul unless one sits and deliberately removes them [the teachings] from one's heart.

Forgetfulness is a natural part of life. Some things are better off being forgotten, others better off being remembered.

The good that we do for others is better off being forgotten, the good that others do for us is better off being remembered and acknowledged.

The wrong we have committed is better to be remembered, the wrong to which we have been subjected is better to be ignored or forgotten.

In the real world, we too often do just the opposite, magnifying our own good deeds and minimizing our deficient actions or words, and minimizing the good deeds of others but maximizing their deficits.

We tend to remember that which is important to us. Certainly God's words are so vital that there is no room for forgetfulness; surely no room for purposeful forgetfulness that is the end result of ascribing less importance to God's word. What is important enough for God to share with us is important enough to keep in our active consciousness.

In marriage, what we perceive to be of importance to our marital partner should by definition become important to us, and therefore more likely to be remembered.

❧ MISHNAH 11 ❧

יא. רַבִּי חֲנִינָא בֶּן דּוֹסָא אוֹמֵר: כֹּל שֶׁיִּרְאַת חֶטְאוֹ קוֹדֶמֶת לְחָכְמָתוֹ, חָכְמָתוֹ מִתְקַיֶּמֶת; וְכֹל שֶׁחָכְמָתוֹ קוֹדֶמֶת לְיִרְאַת חֶטְאוֹ, אֵין חָכְמָתוֹ מִתְקַיֶּמֶת.

Rabbe Hanina the son of Dosa says: One whose fear of sin comes before one's wisdom, that person's wisdom endures; but one whose wisdom comes before one's fear of sin, that person's wisdom does not endure.

It is good to be smart, it is good to be full of wisdom. But it is not good to see wisdom as a stand alone value. Much depends on what one does with that wisdom.

It is important to know and to understand, but not simply for the sake of having knowledge. Knowledge can be used as a tool to put down others, or to justify being arrogantly superior. Such knowledge can often be destructive.

On the other hand, one may approach the quest for knowledge out of the sincere desire to avoid all wrongdoing. The knowledge then fits snugly into the desire to do that which is right and proper.

Knowing all the rules for marriage is important. But even more important is that the desire to know the rules is fueled by the genuine commitment to avoid all wrongdoing, including encroachment on the respect one accords one's spouse.

❧ MISHNAH 12 ❧

יב. הוּא הָיָה אוֹמֵר: כֹּל שֶׁמַּעֲשָׂיו מְרֻבִּין מֵחָכְמָתוֹ, חָכְמָתוֹ מִתְקַיֶּמֶת; וְכֹל
שֶׁחָכְמָתוֹ מְרֻבָּה מִמַּעֲשָׂיו, אֵין חָכְמָתוֹ מִתְקַיֶּמֶת.

He [Rabbe Hanina the son of Dosa] used to say: One whose deeds exceed one's wisdom, that person's wisdom endures; but one whose wisdom exceeds one's deeds, that person's wisdom does not endure.

Another important feature of the quest for wisdom, aside from the context within which one seeks the wisdom, is what one does with the acquired wisdom.

To know, to therefore know what to do, how to behave, but to fail to make that knowledge into a living reality, is to embrace a faulty wisdom that is destined to fail.

Enduring wisdom is wisdom that is put into practice. Meaningful marital wisdom is to know what are one's responsibilities in marriage, and to then implement that knowledge in a caring and sensitive manner.

❧ MISHNAH 13 ❧

יג. הוּא הָיָה אוֹמֵר: כֹּל שֶׁרוּחַ הַבְּרִיּוֹת נוֹחָה הֵימֶנּוּ, רוּחַ הַמָּקוֹם נוֹחָה
הֵימֶנּוּ; וְכֹל שֶׁאֵין רוּחַ הַבְּרִיּוֹת נוֹחָה הֵימֶנּוּ, אֵין רוּחַ הַמָּקוֹם נוֹחָה הֵימֶנּוּ.

*He [Rabbe Hanina the son of Dosa] used to say: One in whom the spirit of
humankind takes delight, the spirit of the Omnipresent takes delight; but
one in whom the spirit of humankind does not take delight, the spirit of the
Omnipresent takes no delight.*

We often wonder whether we are on the right track, whether our
thoughts and actions are acceptable to God; in simple terms, whether
God likes us. If only we could know.

Well, there is a gauge. That gauge is the spirit of humankind. Are
we accepted and appreciated by humans who are spiritually imbued,
humans who have a profound grasp of what is important in life?

Is our behavior in the privacy of our home one that our spouse
genuinely values? If we have achieved that lofty goal, we can surmise
that God likes us.

❧ MISHNAH 14 ❧

יד. רַבִּי דוֹסָא בֶּן הָרְכִּינַס אוֹמֵר: שֵׁנָה שֶׁל שַׁחֲרִית, וְיַיִן שֶׁל צָהֳרַיִם, וְשִׂיחַת הַיְלָדִים וִישִׁיבַת בָּתֵּי כְנֵסִיּוֹת שֶׁל עַמֵּי הָאָרֶץ, מוֹצִיאִין אֶת הָאָדָם מִן הָעוֹלָם.

Rabbe Dosa the son of Hurkenas says: Morning sleep, midday wine, childish talk, and sitting in the assembly houses of the ignorant, drive a person out of the world.

One might question what is wrong with, for example, occasionally sleeping in, or having an afternoon drink.

In truth, very little. A few commentators have remarked that the rare extra sleep, the rare wine, the once in a while kibbitz, is not necessarily bad.

What is not desirable is that these become habits, permanent behavior patterns.

Life is serious, and the occasional banter does not compromise life's seriousness. What is needed is a sense of balance, that the light moments are a very minor part of an otherwise focused life.

That balance of light and serious, in the appropriate proportions, is similarly so conducive to marital harmony.

❧ MISHNAH 15 ❧

טו. רַבִּי אֶלְעָזָר הַמּוֹדָעִי אוֹמֵר: הַמְחַלֵּל אֶת הַקֳּדָשִׁים, וְהַמְבַזֶּה אֶת הַמּוֹעֲדוֹת, וְהַמַּלְבִּין פְּנֵי חֲבֵרוֹ בָּרַבִּים, וְהַמֵּפֵר בְּרִיתוֹ שֶׁל אַבְרָהָם אָבִינוּ, וְהַמְגַלֶּה פָנִים בַּתּוֹרָה שֶׁלֹּא כַהֲלָכָה, אַף עַל פִּי שֶׁיֵּשׁ בְּיָדוֹ תּוֹרָה וּמַעֲשִׂים טוֹבִים, אֵין לוֹ חֵלֶק לָעוֹלָם הַבָּא.

Rabbe Elazar of Modin says: One who profanes sacred things, who despises the appointed festivals, who humiliates a fellow in public, who rejects the covenant of our patriarch Avraham, and who interprets the Torah contradictory to the halakhah [Jewish law], even though in possession of Torah knowledge and good deeds, has no share in the world-to-come.

The common theme here is the appreciation of sanctity. Not all matter is the same. Some things are sacred. Not all days are the same; some days are sacred. Human beings are sacred. The covenant places upon us sacred responsibilities. And the Torah is not just another book. It is sacred.

Sanctity creates its own frame of obligation and appreciation. Treating everything the same removes us from sanctity and sacred responsibility, severely compromising how we approach life.

In the realm of relationships, the same may be said about marriage. All relationships are important, but the sacred responsibilities of marriage are unique, because marriage is a distinctively holy relationship.

Other relationships, other friendships can range from ordinary to outstanding. But there is no room for ordinariness in marriage.

❧ MISHNAH 16 ❧

טז. רַבִּי יִשְׁמָעֵאל אוֹמֵר: הֱוֵי קַל לְרֹאשׁ, וְנוֹחַ לְתִשְׁחוֹרֶת, וֶהֱוֵי מְקַבֵּל אֶת כָּל הָאָדָם בְּשִׂמְחָה.

Rabbe Yishmael says: Be amenable with a superior, co-operative with youth, and receive all people with cheerfulness.

The bottom line is that our dealings with people should rest on a foundation of happiness for the opportunity to interact.

But how we interact differs. The way we interact with younger people is not the same as the way we interact with older people, or with those to whom we have to answer.

Interaction is not a one-size-fits-all generic approach. We need to recognize the situation, and the person, and react accordingly, with thoughtfulness and sensitivity.

That type of approach in marriage is so helpful. The challenge of today is not necessarily the same as the challenge of yesterday. The mood of the marital partner today may be different than it was yesterday.

Be aware, be alert, be caring in the approach, rather than reacting by reflex.

✤ MISHNAH 17 ✤

יז. רַבִּי עֲקִיבָא אוֹמֵר: שְׂחוֹק וְקַלּוּת רֹאשׁ מַרְגִּילִין אֶת הָאָדָם לְעֶרְוָה. מָסֹרֶת סְיָג לַתּוֹרָה, מַעַשְׂרוֹת סְיָג לָעֹשֶׁר, נְדָרִים סְיָג לִפְרִישׁוּת, סְיָג לַחָכְמָה שְׁתִיקָה.

Rabbe Akiva says: Jesting and levity accustom a person to lewdness. The transmitted tradition is a hedge around the Torah, tithes are a hedge for wealth, vows are hedge for abstinence, and a hedge for wisdom is silence.

Behavior control is so vital to preventing a person from going off track. It is therefore important, as a first step, to be serious about life rather than being light-headed.

Having boundaries to prevent even inadvertent deviation is a further guard from veering off track. Mis-step regarding observance is more likely to be avoided by following the Rabbinic guidelines on fulfilling the Torah.

Sharing through tithing helps avoid an obsessional desire to acquire and devour. Firm resolve in the form of strong undertaking can help control impulse, and saying nothing is an almost fool-proof way to avoid saying something stupid.

The potential pitfalls that inhere in marriage itself can likewise be prevented through pre-emptive strategies that anticipate looming issues.

Going the extra step rather than merely fulfilling one's obligation is most helpful. So is genuine sharing, as well as true commitment to doing one's best.

Finally, silence, which leads to meaningful listening and understanding, goes a long way toward better appreciating issues and fixing them.

❦ MISHNAH 18 ❦

יח. הוּא הָיָה אוֹמֵר: חָבִיב אָדָם שֶׁנִּבְרָא בְּצֶלֶם, חִבָּה יְתֵרָה נוֹדַעַת לוֹ
שֶׁנִּבְרָא בְּצֶלֶם, שֶׁנֶּאֱמַר: כִּי בְּצֶלֶם אֱלֹהִים עָשָׂה אֶת הָאָדָם. חֲבִיבִין יִשְׂרָאֵל
שֶׁנִּקְרְאוּ בָנִים לַמָּקוֹם, חִבָּה יְתֵרָה נוֹדַעַת לָהֶם שֶׁנִּקְרְאוּ בָנִים לַמָּקוֹם,
שֶׁנֶּאֱמַר: בָּנִים אַתֶּם לַייָ אֱלֹהֵיכֶם. חֲבִיבִין יִשְׂרָאֵל שֶׁנִּתַּן לָהֶם כְּלִי חֶמְדָּה,
חִבָּה יְתֵרָה נוֹדַעַת לָהֶם שֶׁנִּתַּן לָהֶם כְּלִי חֶמְדָּה, שֶׁנֶּאֱמַר: כִּי לֶקַח טוֹב
נָתַתִּי לָכֶם, תּוֹרָתִי אַל תַּעֲזֹבוּ.

*He [Rabbe Akiva] used to say: Beloved is the human being, as he was created
in God's image; greater is that love in that it was made known to him that
he was created in God's image, as it is said – "for in the image of God did
God make the person"* (BERESHIS 9:6). *Beloved are Israel as they are called
children of the Omnipresent; greater is that love in that it was made known
to them that they are called children of the Omnipresent, as it is said – "You
are children to the Lord your God . . ."* (DEVARIM 14:1). *Beloved are Israel,
as a precious instrument was given to them; greater is that love in that it
was made known to them that a precious instrument was given to them via
which the world was created, as it is said – "For I gave you a good doctrine,
forsake not My Torah"* (MISHLAY 4:2).

A marital relationship, however good it is, can always be better.

An easy way to make a good relationship better is by making it
known to one's spouse how much they are loved and appreciated.

Such expression gives an extra dimension to the love. It con-
veys a strong sense of being truly valued rather than being taken for
granted.

Of course, the words must be backed up by actions which show
quite concretely that the words are not hollow platitudes. Bottom
line – not only seeing, but also hearing, is believing.

❧ MISHNAH 19 ❧

יט. הַכֹּל צָפוּי, וְהָרְשׁוּת נְתוּנָה, וּבְטוֹב הָעוֹלָם נִדּוֹן, וְהַכֹּל לְפִי רוֹב הַמַּעֲשֶׂה.

*All is foreseen yet freedom [of choice] is given, the world is judged according
to the good, and everything is measured by the multitude of deeds.*

The more good deeds, the better; for the world, and surely for the
world of marriage.

Whatever destiny the marriage may have, it remains in our hands
to define it, by our actions and reactions.

In the positive realm, it is in our hands to initiate nice thoughts
and actions, and to reciprocate such niceness.

On the less positive side, how we react to being neglected, or
perhaps being yelled at, is likewise in our hands. There is no law that
says we must scream back, or sulk.

We best exercise our humanity by choosing to rise above the
potential fray, and thereby heading off a crisis.

❧ MISHNAH 20 ❧

כ. הוּא הָיָה אוֹמֵר: הַכֹּל נָתוּן בְּעֵרָבוֹן, וּמְצוּדָה פְרוּסָה עַל כָּל הַחַיִּים. הֶחָנוּת פְּתוּחָה, וְהַחֶנְוָנִי מַקִּיף, וְהַפִּנְקָס פָּתוּחַ, וְהַיָּד כּוֹתֶבֶת, וְכָל הָרוֹצֶה לִלְווֹת יָבֹא וְיִלְוֶה. וְהַגַּבָּאִין מַחֲזִירִין תָּדִיר בְּכָל יוֹם, וְנִפְרָעִין מִן הָאָדָם מִדַּעְתּוֹ וְשֶׁלֹּא מִדַּעְתּוֹ. וְיֵשׁ לָהֶם עַל מַה שֶּׁיִּסְמֹכוּ, וְהַדִּין דִּין אֱמֶת, וְהַכֹּל מְתֻקָּן לִסְעוּדָה.

He [Rabbe Akiva] used to say: Everything is given on pledge, and a net is spread out over all the living. The store is open, the merchant extends credit, the ledger is open, and the hand writes; whoever wishes to borrow may come and borrow. The collectors regularly make their rounds each day, and they exact payment from the person whether with or without that person's knowledge. They have what to rely on, the judgment is a true judgment, and all is ready for the banquet.

In the give-and-take that unfolds in relationships, including marriage, it is best if everyone is full of understanding and compassion, grateful for the good, and ready to forgive and forget trespass.

That is the way for each of the marriage partners to approach themselves. It is not the way of marriage partners to demand, or even expect that of the other.

Instead, the marriage works best when each places high demands not on the other, but on themselves.

Good deeds will help fatten the account, but no one should go into the relationship expecting the other to understand. Each is best off setting a high bar for themselves, demanding more of themselves rather than less, being sure to act properly rather than accepting mediocrity, if not worse.

The more demanding we are on ourselves, the better the outcome. No bargains, no shortcuts; just expecting that all of our actions have logical consequences.

❧ MISHNAH 21 ❧

כא. רַבִּי אֶלְעָזָר בֶּן עֲזַרְיָה אוֹמֵר: אִם אֵין תּוֹרָה אֵין דֶּרֶךְ אֶרֶץ, אִם אֵין
דֶּרֶךְ אֶרֶץ אֵין תּוֹרָה; אִם אֵין חָכְמָה אֵין יִרְאָה, אִם אֵין יִרְאָה אֵין חָכְמָה;
אִם אֵין דַּעַת אֵין בִּינָה, אִם אֵין בִּינָה אֵין דַּעַת; אִם אֵין קֶמַח אֵין תּוֹרָה,
אִם אֵין תּוֹרָה אֵין קֶמַח.

Rabbe Elazar the son of Azarya says: If there is no Torah, there is no
proper conduct; if there is no proper conduct, there is no Torah. If there is
no wisdom, there is no awe; if there is no awe, there is no wisdom. If there is
no knowledge, there is no understanding; if there is no understanding, there
is no knowledge. If there is no sustenance, there is no Torah; if there is no
Torah, there is no sustenance.

The theme in this Mishnah is the complementary nature of some
values, that one cannot function without the other.

The Torah teaches how to behave. Without the Torah, behavior is
deficient. Behavior that is lacking diminishes from Torah.

Wisdom about the true nature of life cannot be realized if it is not
combined with being in awe of life. Awe itself is only true awe if it
inspires toward wisdom.

Without knowledge of the facts, one cannot truly understand.
Decisions made in ignorance are poor decisions. Without understanding, it is clear that there is a knowledge deficit.

Finally, one needs the wherewithal to live in order to fulfill the
Torah, but just living without Torah-imbued meaning is not real living;
it is just existing.

In the marriage ideal, each brings to the marital entity the complementary values that make the union into a fully vibrant completeness,
a sustaining dynamism of awe-inspired wisdom rooted in Torah
principles.

❧ MISHNAH 22 ❧

כב. הוּא הָיָה אוֹמֵר: כֹּל שֶׁחָכְמָתוֹ מְרֻבָּה מִמַּעֲשָׂיו, לְמָה הוּא דוֹמֶה: לְאִילָן שֶׁעֲנָפָיו מְרֻבִּין וְשָׁרָשָׁיו מוּעָטִין, וְהָרוּחַ בָּאָה וְעוֹקַרְתּוֹ וְהוֹפַכְתּוֹ עַל פָּנָיו, שֶׁנֶּאֱמַר: וְהָיָה כְּעַרְעָר בָּעֲרָבָה, וְלֹא יִרְאֶה כִּי יָבֹא טוֹב, וְשָׁכַן חֲרֵרִים בַּמִּדְבָּר, אֶרֶץ מְלֵחָה וְלֹא תֵשֵׁב. אֲבָל כֹּל שֶׁמַּעֲשָׂיו מְרֻבִּין מֵחָכְמָתוֹ, לְמָה הוּא דוֹמֶה: לְאִילָן שֶׁעֲנָפָיו מוּעָטִין וְשָׁרָשָׁיו מְרֻבִּין, שֶׁאֲפִילוּ כָל הָרוּחוֹת שֶׁבָּעוֹלָם בָּאוֹת וְנוֹשְׁבוֹת בּוֹ, אֵין מְזִיזִין אוֹתוֹ מִמְּקוֹמוֹ, שֶׁנֶּאֱמַר: וְהָיָה כְּעֵץ שָׁתוּל עַל מַיִם, וְעַל יוּבַל יְשַׁלַּח שָׁרָשָׁיו, וְלֹא יִרְאֶה כִּי יָבֹא חֹם, וְהָיָה עָלֵהוּ רַעֲנָן, וּבִשְׁנַת בַּצֹּרֶת לֹא יִדְאָג, וְלֹא יָמִישׁ מֵעֲשׂוֹת פֶּרִי.

He [Rabbe Elazar the son of Azarya] used to say: One whose wisdom exceeds one's deeds, to what is that person comparable? To a tree whose branches are many but whose roots are few, that the wind comes and uproots it and overturns it upon its face, as it is said – "He will be like a lonely tree in the wasteland and will not see when good comes, but will inhabit the parched places of the wilderness, a salt filled land which is uninhabitable" (YIRMIYAHU 17:6). *But one whose deeds exceed one's wisdom, to what is that person comparable? To a tree whose branches are few but whose roots are many, so that even if all the winds in the world would come and blow upon it, they would not move it from its place, as it is said – "He shall be like a tree planted by the waters, which spreads out its roots by the river, and shall not sense when heat comes but its foliage shall remain fresh; it will not be troubled in the year of drought, nor will it cease to bear fruit"* (YIRMIYAHU 17:8).

To know what to do, but to fail in fully implementing that knowledge, is to relegate that knowledge to the realm of the theoretical. The knowledge is there, but it is not reinforced by the necessary action.

On the other hand, knowledge that is reinforced by the deeds that flow from the knowledge entrenches that knowledge as the root source of life.

A couple whose values are firmly rooted, who live these values, will create a home of trust and strength that can withstand the challenges that inevitably come to the fore.

❧ MISHNAH 23 ❧

כג. רַבִּי אֱלִיעֶזֶר חִסְמָא אוֹמֵר: קִנִּין וּפִתְחֵי נִדָּה, הֵן הֵן גּוּפֵי הֲלָכוֹת. תְּקוּפוֹת וְגִמַּטְרִיָּאוֹת, פַּרְפְּרָאוֹת לַחָכְמָה.

Rabbe Elazar Hisma says: The rules of bird offerings and the onset of menstruation are essential ordinances of the law. Astronomy and geometry are mere after-courses of wisdom.

This Mishnah seems to be totally out of place. There is hardly an ethical principle in this observation. And the observation itself seems to have no higher implication.

What may be at work here is an interesting comment on the issue of relevance. The bird offering rules and the details regarding menstruation are quire complex and detailed. They hardly seem like topics that directly impact on one's life.

But in studying them, one cannot help but be impressed with the meticulous details involved. The actual application of these details may be far-fetched, but that is not the point. What is crucial is that details, however minute, are integral to our fully appreciating the Torah.

Astronomy and geometry are important, but hardly impact on life. They give life an interesting and inviting flavor, like a good dessert. But the main course is the detail which we uncover in every nuance of our daily life.

Seeing the beauty and importance of all the details, the attentiveness we apply to even the small matters of the marital relationship, spill over quite wonderfully into all aspects of the marriage, even if we do not realize it at the moment.

Chapter Four

❧ MISHNAH 1 ❧

א. בֶּן זוֹמָא אוֹמֵר: אֵיזֶהוּ חָכָם, הַלּוֹמֵד מִכָּל אָדָם, שֶׁנֶּאֱמַר: מִכָּל מְלַמְּדַי
הִשְׂכַּלְתִּי, כִּי עֵדְוֹתֶיךָ שִׂיחָה לִי. אֵיזֶהוּ גִבּוֹר, הַכּוֹבֵשׁ אֶת יִצְרוֹ, שֶׁנֶּאֱמַר:
טוֹב אֶרֶךְ אַפַּיִם מִגִּבּוֹר וּמוֹשֵׁל בְּרוּחוֹ מִלֹּכֵד עִיר. אֵיזֶהוּ עָשִׁיר, הַשָּׂמֵחַ
בְּחֶלְקוֹ, שֶׁנֶּאֱמַר: יְגִיעַ כַּפֶּיךָ כִּי תֹאכֵל, אַשְׁרֶיךָ וְטוֹב לָךְ - אַשְׁרֶיךָ בָּעוֹלָם
הַזֶּה, וְטוֹב לָךְ לָעוֹלָם הַבָּא. אֵיזֶהוּ מְכֻבָּד, הַמְכַבֵּד אֶת הַבְּרִיּוֹת, שֶׁנֶּאֱמַר:
כִּי מְכַבְּדַי אֲכַבֵּד וּבֹזַי יֵקָלּוּ.

Ben Zoma says: Who is wise? One who learns from all people, as it is said –
"From all those who have taught me I have obtained understanding, for Your
testimonies are conversation for me" (TEHILLIM 119:99). *Who is mighty?*
One who conquers one's passions, as it is written – "One who is slow to anger
is better than a mighty person, and one who rules over one's spirit is better
than one who conquers a city" (MISHLAY 16:32). *Who is rich? One who*
rejoices in one's portion, as it is said – "When you eat of the labor of your
hands, you are praiseworthy and it is well with you" (TEHILLIM 128:2).
You are praiseworthy – in this world; and it is well with you– in the world
to come. Who is honored? One who honors humankind, as it is said – "for
those who honor Me I will honor, and those who despise Me shall be held in
contempt" (I SHMUEL 2:30).

This Mishnah is a wonderful paradigm for marriage.

It is vital to never think you know everything about your spouse.
Continue to learn more about your spouse, so you can be ever more
attentive and responsive.

There are different ways that passion impacts on the marital

73

relationship. One may feel more comfortable to let loose in anger at one's marital partner. We are called upon to be mighty, to overcome that easily available but destructive desire.

Or it could refer to the passion in the relationship which, if devoid of control, can lead to abuse in the obsessive pursuit of one's desires. We are to be mighty, to conquer that passion; to focus, in love, on one's marital partner rather than on fulfilling one's desires. In such self-transcendence, in concentrating on "the" other, one ironically fulfills one's own self.

To be happy with one's marital partner rather than thinking that there might be a better partner somewhere is at the root of marital harmony. You and your partner are as one. Accepting that, and building upon that, is the foundation for marital bliss.

Finally, genuinely bestowing honor on one's spouse is the best guarantor that the honor will be reciprocated. The genuine quality inheres in bestowing honor not for the sake of a reward, but simply because it is the correct approach to marriage. The rest follows naturally, absent demands or expectations.

✤ MISHNAH 2 ✤

ב. בֶּן עַזַּאי אוֹמֵר: הֱוֵי רָץ לְמִצְוָה קַלָּה, וּבוֹרֵחַ מִן הָעֲבֵרָה, שֶׁמִּצְוָה גוֹרֶרֶת מִצְוָה, וַעֲבֵרָה גוֹרֶרֶת עֲבֵרָה; שֶׁשְּׂכַר מִצְוָה מִצְוָה, וּשְׂכַר עֲבֵרָה עֲבֵרָה.

Ben Azzai says: Hasten to fulfill even a light precept, and flee from all sin, since one good deed generates another good deed and one sin generates another sin; for the recompense for a good deed is a good deed and the recompense for a sin is a sin.

Small kindnesses, what may seem like minor expressions of love and concern, generate significant impact. Doing good generates doing more good, both by the partner generating the goodness and by the recipient spouse.

This sets into motion an upward spiral toward more goodness and kindness that brings out the best in each other.

Unfortunately, the same generating principle can work in reverse. Neglect, careless actions or remarks, work in the opposite direction, causing more negative reaction, either consciously or unconsciously, and launching a downward spiral in the relationship.

Every deed, however small, has potentially large implications.

❧ MISHNAH 3 ❧

ג. הוּא הָיָה אוֹמֵר: אַל תְּהִי בָז לְכָל אָדָם וְאַל תְּהִי מַפְלִיג לְכָל דָּבָר,
שֶׁאֵין לְךָ אָדָם שֶׁאֵין לוֹ שָׁעָה, וְאֵין לְךָ דָּבָר שֶׁאֵין לוֹ מָקוֹם.

*He [Ben Azzai] used to say: Do not despise any person and do not consider
anything impossible, for there is no person who does not have an hour and
no thing that does not have its place.*

Unfortunately, not every marriage succeeds. And of those that do not,
there are varying degrees of failure, ranging from relatively peaceful
to intensely harsh and contentious.

In the harsh divorce, there is harsh language, with accusations and
bitterness more associated with real enemies.

As difficult as it may be, this statement of Ben Azzai is worth
applying specifically to situations when despising is likely to ensue.

Divorce can lead to despising, despising can lead to divorce. As
much as divorce is an undesirable reality, once it happens it is best to
move on, and to not allow hatred to fester within.

In the end, it is the person who harbors the hatred who suffers the
most. Even when one can be excused for holding on to such negative
feelings, still it is not advisable to do so.

✤ MISHNAH 4 ✤

ד. רַבִּי לְוִיטַס אִישׁ יַבְנֶה אוֹמֵר: מְאֹד מְאֹד הֱוֵי שְׁפַל רוּחַ, שֶׁתִּקְוַת אֱנוֹשׁ רִמָּה.

Rabbe Levitas of Yavneh says: Be of an exceedingly humble spirit, for the hope of the human being is decay.

Humility is a wonderful trait at all times, including marriage. Yes, it is very heartening when each of the marriage partners considers their counterpart to be the greatest.

At the same time, it is disheartening, even downright depressing, when either of the partners considers their own self to be the greatest.

With an "I am the greatest" attitude comes the less than explicit but nevertheless quite evident attitude of "I am always right."

Having such an attitude is a recipe for marriage disaster, as the "greatest" will find it unbecoming to admit being wrong and to apologize. Then comes digging in the heels, refusal to budge, accusations and counter-accusations, leading to the collapse of the marriage, a collapse than could have, and would have been avoided had humility been present.

ה. רַבִּי יוֹחָנָן בֶּן בְּרוֹקָה אוֹמֵר: כָּל הַמְחַלֵּל שֵׁם שָׁמַיִם בַּסֵּתֶר, נִפְרָעִין מִמֶּנּוּ בְּגָלוּי; אֶחָד שׁוֹגֵג וְאֶחָד מֵזִיד בְּחִלּוּל הַשֵּׁם.

Rabbe Yohanan the son of Beroka says: Whoever desecrates the name of God in private will suffer the penalty in public. Whether unwittingly or wittingly, it is the same concerning desecration of the Name.

There are different ways to desecrate the Name of God in private. In the realm of marriage, one who desecrates God's Name in the privacy of the marital home, behaving contrary to the sacred obligations that inhere to marriage, may think that this behavior is a private matter.

It may begin as a private matter, but it eventually spills out into the public, through a slip of the tongue, or more physical manifestations of abusive behavior.

The undertakings in marriage are such that there is no room for neglect. Getting married comes with contractual obligations, including to convey the preciousness of one's spouse at all times. Anything less is a dereliction of duty.

Witting or unwitting, it is all the same; such is the seriousness of the marital contract. Desecrating the marital compact is the desecration of a Godly responsibility that can hardly be contained, any more than true human emotions and feelings can be contained and stifled.

✤ MISHNAH 6 ✤

ו. רַבִּי יִשְׁמָעֵאל בַּר רַבִּי יוֹסֵי אוֹמֵר: הַלּוֹמֵד תּוֹרָה עַל מְנָת לְלַמֵּד, מַסְפִּיקִין בְּיָדוֹ לִלְמוֹד וּלְלַמֵּד; וְהַלּוֹמֵד עַל מְנָת לַעֲשׂוֹת, מַסְפִּיקִין בְּיָדוֹ לִלְמוֹד וּלְלַמֵּד, לִשְׁמוֹר וְלַעֲשׂוֹת.

Rabbe Yishmael the son of Rabbe Yose says: One who studies Torah in order to teach will be granted the opportunity to study and to teach; and one who studies in order to practice will be granted the opportunity to learn and to teach, to observe and to fulfill.

Limited horizons bring limited fulfillments. Stretched horizons yield more significant results.

Learning in order to be able to teach is certainly a worthy aspiration, but not nearly as worthy as studying in order move the study from theoretical to actual.

In preparing for marriage, both before marriage and during the marriage, it is important to know what are one's obligations.

Even more crucial is absorbing all that knowledge with the full intent and determination to carry out those obligations to the full.

With such an attitude, the marriage is destined to be most fulfilling.

❧ MISHNAH 7 ❧

ז. רַבִּי צָדוֹק אוֹמֵר: אַל תִּפְרוֹשׁ מִן הַצִּבּוּר, וְאַל תַּעַשׂ עַצְמְךָ כְּעוֹרְכֵי הַדַּיָּנִין, וְאַל תַּעֲשֶׂהָ עֲטָרָה לְהִתְגַּדֵּל בָּהּ, וְלֹא קַרְדּוֹם לַחְפּוֹר בָּהּ. וְכַךְ הָיָה הִלֵּל אוֹמֵר: וּדְאִשְׁתַּמֵּשׁ בְּתַגָּא חֲלָף; הָא לָמַדְתָּ, כָּל הַנֶּהֱנֶה מִדִּבְרֵי תוֹרָה, נוֹטֵל חַיָּיו מִן הָעוֹלָם.

*Rabbe Zadok says: Do not separate from the community; in the posi-
tion of judge do not act as counsel; do not make of the Torah a crown for
self-aggrandizement nor a spade wherewith to dig. And so Hillel used to
say – "One who makes use of the crown will die." Thus you may derive that
whoever reaps personal profit from the words of the Torah takes one's life
from the world.*

A couple who are happy together are in a wonderful space. As happy
as they are with each other, they are still urged to share their happiness
bounty with the community, even if it is simply by being part of the
community.

    In being part of the community, perhaps in the desire to spread
good cheer, one may step out of bounds, such as by overstepping one's
role as a judge in order to give lawyer-type advice to a person about
to stand in judgement. It is nice to want to be helpful, specially when
one feels blessed, but helpfulness must not intrude onto fairness.

    Likewise, the involvement with the community should be with the
strong desire to share, rather than the desire for self-gain.

❧ MISHNAH 8 ❧

ח. רַבִּי יוֹסֵי אוֹמֵר: כָּל הַמְכַבֵּד אֶת הַתּוֹרָה, גּוּפוֹ מְכֻבָּד עַל הַבְּרִיּוֹת; וְכָל
הַמְחַלֵּל אֶת הַתּוֹרָה, גּוּפוֹ מְחֻלָּל עַל הַבְּרִיּוֹת.

Rabbe Yose says: Whoever honors the Torah will be honored by humankind,
but whoever profanes the Torah will be rejected by humankind.

The dynamic suggested in this Mishnah is that our actions, for better or
for worse, generate commensurate reactions. By extending honor, the
honor reflects back. By being disrespectful, that disrespect bounces
back on the perpetrator.

This applies to how we approach the actualization of Torah values.
One of those values is the sanctity of marriage, the mitzvah obligation
to gladden our spouse, directed primarily to the husband for his wife,
but also from the wife to her husband.

Honor genuinely bestowed is likely to become honor reciprocated,
and disrespect is also likely to boomerang.

❧ MISHNAH 9 ❧

ט. רַבִּי יִשְׁמָעֵאל בְּנוֹ אוֹמֵר: הַחֹשֵׂךְ עַצְמוֹ מִן הַדִּין, פּוֹרֵק מִמֶּנּוּ אֵיבָה וְגָזֵל
וּשְׁבוּעַת שָׁוְא. וְהַגַּס לִבּוֹ בְּהוֹרָאָה – שׁוֹטֶה, רָשָׁע, וְגַס רוּחַ.

*Rabbi Yishmael his [Rabbe Yose's] son says: One who avoids assuming
judicial office rids the self of hatred, robbery, and vain swearing. And one
who renders decisions presumptuously is foolish, wicked, and arrogant.*

One is here cautioned to be careful about rushing to be a judge. It
seems like a lofty position, but has its pitfalls, both in the very nature
of what transpires in court, and in what happens to someone who
becomes infatuated with the eagerness to judge.

But the advice to steer clear of being judgmental also applies to the
way we relate to people out of court. For example, being judgmental
of one's marital partner is not conducive to marital harmony.

The moment one sits in judgment, one has upset the delicate
marital balance, from one of equals, to a relationship of a higher and
a lower, of one who judges and one who is being judged.

The chances of such a marriage being harmonious are severely
compromised by this rush to exercise judgment.

❧ MISHNAH 10 ❧

י. הוּא הָיָה אוֹמֵר: אַל תְּהִי דָן יְחִידִי, שֶׁאֵין דָּן יְחִידִי אֶלָּא אֶחָד; וְאַל תֹּאמַר
קַבְּלוּ דַעְתִּי, שֶׁהֵן רַשָּׁאִין וְלֹא אָתָּה.

*He [Rabbe Yishmael] used to say: Do not judge alone, for none may judge
alone except One; and do not say – "accept my opinion," for it is their choice,
not yours.*

Applied to marriage, this is an exhortation to work in tandem, for husband and wife to operate as a team, and to make decisions together.

Neither should impose a decision on the other, and instead should
assure that there is agreement and comfort with the decisions being
made.

Neither is the boss of the house, and the insistence on mutuality
should not have to come as a demand of the one to the other.

Instead, it should come as the insistence of the one that the other
be an equal partner in the decision making.

❧ MISHNAH 11 ❧

יא. רַבִּי יוֹנָתָן אוֹמֵר: כָּל הַמְקַיֵּם אֶת הַתּוֹרָה מֵעֹנִי, סוֹפוֹ לְקַיְּמָהּ מֵעֹשֶׁר;
וְכָל הַמְבַטֵּל אֶת הַתּוֹרָה מֵעֹשֶׁר, סוֹפוֹ לְבַטְּלָהּ מֵעֹנִי.

*Rabbe Yonatan says: Whoever fulfills the Torah out of poverty will ulti-
mately fulfill it out of wealth, but whoever neglects the Torah out of wealth
will eventually neglect the Torah out of poverty.*

One of the messages that derive from this Mishnah is that the priorities
we set for ourselves should be based on their inherent value, and not
on our circumstances.

Fulfilling Torah is critically important, and using our circumstance
as an excuse to neglect it is just that – an excuse. Poverty does not
negate the ability to fulfill the Torah, nor does the pursuit of wealth,
whatever the noble justification for such pursuit, excuse one from
fulfilling the Torah.

So it is with establishing the obligation to one's spouse as uncon-
ditionally important, as independent of circumstance. Whatever one's
means, the spouse is priority.

❧ MISHNAH 12 ❧

יב. רַבִּי מֵאִיר אוֹמֵר: הֱוֵי מְמַעֵט בְּעֵסֶק וַעֲסוֹק בַּתּוֹרָה, וֶהֱוֵי שְׁפַל רוּחַ בִּפְנֵי כָל אָדָם. וְאִם בָּטַלְתָּ מִן הַתּוֹרָה, יֶשׁ לְךָ בְּטֵלִים הַרְבֵּה כְּנֶגְדֶּךָ, וְאִם עָמַלְתָּ בַּתּוֹרָה הַרְבֵּה, יֶשׁ לוֹ שָׂכָר הַרְבֵּה לִתֶּן לָךְ.

Rabbe Meir says: Minimize your business activities and occupy yourself with Torah, and be of humble spirit before all people. If you neglect the Torah many causes for neglecting the Torah will present themselves to you, but if you toil in the Torah God has much recompense to give you.

Exactly how one strikes a balance between business pursuits and Torah pursuits is a delicate process.

As much as the end goal is clear, as much as the fulfillment of Torah values is the highest endeavor, nevertheless both pursuits have their place.

Rabbe Meir is clearly not suggesting that one drop all business pursuits; rather that one minimize, one cut down the time devoted to business pursuits little by little, so that one does not, in haste, actually be left with no income.

Not everyone is in the same position, so if one is able to minimize but someone else not as able to do so, this is not cause to gloat. It may simply be a matter of differing circumstances leading to different abilities. Therefore, be of humble spirit.

There will always be excuses to justify one's actions. The important aspect of this realization of life balance is to approach it honestly and fairly, with resolve and with full appreciation of one's realistic abilities.

Simultaneously, this a most worthwhile manner of approaching one's responsibility to one's marital partner – being methodical and mindful of what is at stake.

❧ MISHNAH 13 ❧

יג. רַבִּי אֱלִיעֶזֶר בֶּן יַעֲקֹב אוֹמֵר: הָעוֹשֶׂה מִצְוָה אַחַת, קוֹנֶה לוֹ פְּרַקְלִיט אֶחָד, וְהָעוֹבֵר עֲבֵרָה אַחַת, קוֹנֶה לוֹ קַטֵּגוֹר אֶחָד. תְּשׁוּבָה וּמַעֲשִׂים טוֹבִים כִּתְרִיס בִּפְנֵי הַפּוּרְעָנוּת.

Rabbe Eliezer the son of Yaakov says: One who fulfills one precept gains for the self one advocate, and one who commits one transgression gets for the self one accuser. Repentance and good deeds are as a shield against calamity.

Every deed makes a difference, every action has a consequence. The good that we are able to achieve reflects on who we are, as does the contrary behavior.

These are our choices, for which we take full ownership. We land up owning advocates and accusers, depending on what choices we make. This works for the fullness of life, including, of course, the deeds that define the marital union.

We are human, and we are prone to err, to transgress. To be mired in the transgression is to compound the error and make matters worse.

It is therefore of utmost importance to make amends if one has erred; if one has acted less than nicely toward one's spouse.

Amends take the form of repenting for the error, and replacing the transgression with good deeds. That will stop the bleeding and start the healing.

✤ MISHNAH 14 ✤

יד. רַבִּי יוֹחָנָן הַסַּנְדְּלָר אוֹמֵר: כָּל כְּנֵסִיָּה שֶׁהִיא לְשֵׁם שָׁמַיִם סוֹפָהּ לְהִתְקַיֵּם,
וְשֶׁאֵינָהּ לְשֵׁם שָׁמַיִם אֵין סוֹפָהּ לְהִתְקַיֵּם.

Rabbe Yohanan the sandal maker says: Every assembly that is for the sake of Heaven will ultimately endure, but that which is not for the sake of Heaven will ultimately not endure.

An assembly of two united in marriage is more likely to endure if the union is based on motives that are higher than mere self-fulfillment.

If the relationship is moving forward to fulfill a higher purpose, this means it is not a relationship of mutual narcissism. A mutually narcissistic union can move forward, but is absent an enduring quality, and is likely to run into roadblocks when the desires that each of the partners seek to fulfill are not realized.

The higher purpose brings the couple into a higher dimension, into the dimension of self-transcendence, wherein the objective is the realization of higher values; for the sake of Heaven.

Yes, the self is fulfilled, but not as an end goal. Instead, the self is fulfilled precisely through aspiring to loftier goals.

❧ MISHNAH 15 ❧

טו. רַבִּי אֶלְעָזָר בֶּן שַׁמּוּעַ אוֹמֵר: יְהִי כְבוֹד תַּלְמִידְךָ חָבִיב עָלֶיךָ כְּשֶׁלָּךְ,
וּכְבוֹד חֲבֵרְךָ כְּמוֹרָא רַבָּךְ, וּמוֹרָא רַבָּךְ כְּמוֹרָא שָׁמָיִם.

*Rabbe Elazar the son of Shammua says: Let the honor of your disciple be as
dear to you as your own, the honor of your colleague as dear to you as the
reverence for your teacher, and the reverence for your teacher as dear to
you as the awe of Heaven.*

Marriage exists in many dimensions. Ideally, the marriage is one of
equals who interact on many levels.

The couple invariably teach each other by the natural way they
behave, by the values they live, by the respectfulness of their speech,
by their devotion to each other.

In an ideal union, each of the marital partners is a combination of
teacher, colleague, and student.

That the marriage is thus filled with honor and reverence for each
other is a most welcome reality.

❧ MISHNAH 16 ❧

טז. רַבִּי יְהוּדָה אוֹמֵר: הֱוֵי זָהִיר בְּתַלְמוּד, שֶׁשִּׁגְגַת תַּלְמוּד עוֹלָה זָדוֹן.

Rabbe Yehuda says: Be careful in study, for error in study is considered intentional sin.

This Mishnah is so important when approaching marriage. Marriage is about a sacred relationship.

The sanctity of the relationship comes through in the proliferation of rules and guidelines governing marriage.

Aside from the regulations that apply to all relationships, there are ones that are unique to marriage, including obligations to be extra caring and sensitive.

Entry into marriage demands that we be careful in advance, knowing what is expected and necessary for the marriage to flourish.

Lack of care in this regard is more than negligence. Due to the serious nature of marriage, failure to know the responsibilities is tantamount to intentional dereliction.

❧ MISHNAH 17 ❧

יז. רַבִּי שִׁמְעוֹן אוֹמֵר: שְׁלֹשָׁה כְתָרִים הֵן – כֶּתֶר תּוֹרָה, וְכֶתֶר כְּהֻנָּה, וְכֶתֶר מַלְכוּת; וְכֶתֶר שֵׁם טוֹב עוֹלֶה עַל גַּבֵּיהֶן.

Rabbe Shimon says: There are three crowns – the crown of Torah, the crown of priesthood, and the crown of royalty; but the crown of a good name is superimposed upon them all.

Everyone who enters into marriage comes with some pedigree. It could be the pedigree of personal achievement, it could be the pedigree of family lineage, it could a combination of the two.

But overarching these crowns, fitting on top of them, is the crown of a good name, the crown of appreciation from one's spouse for living up to one's sacred marital obligations.

This is an earned crown, and therefore most worthy of distinction.

❧ MISHNAH 18 ❧

יח. רַבִּי נְהוֹרַאי אוֹמֵר: הֱוֵי גוֹלֶה לִמְקוֹם תּוֹרָה, וְאַל תּאֹמַר שֶׁהִיא תָבוֹא אַחֲרֶיךָ, שֶׁחֲבֵרֶיךָ יְקַיְמוּהָ בְיָדֶךָ, וְאֶל בִּינָתְךָ אַל תִּשָּׁעֵן.

Rabbe Nehorai says: Transport yourself to a place of Torah and do not say that it will follow you, for it is your colleagues who will firmly establish it for you, and do not rely on your own understanding.

The climactic last words of this Mishnah speak to how much we need others in order to live up to our obligations.

There is no escaping from the duty to study, to learn, to know, and then to apply, to implement.

Knowing all that goes in to a blissful marriage is critical. But it always helps to seek out others who can help improve our understanding. Trusted colleagues help with our attaining more complete understanding, both in advance of marriage, and during marriage.

Unanticipated situations may arise, potential crises may loom, and the help of those who have the benefit of greater wisdom and experience is always worth seeking.

❧ MISHNAH 19 ❧

יט. רַבִּי יַנַּאי אוֹמֵר: אֵין בְּיָדֵינוּ לֹא מִשַּׁלְוַת הָרְשָׁעִים, וְאַף לֹא מִיִּסּוּרֵי הַצַּדִּיקִים.

Rabbe Yannai says: It is not within our grasp to explain the tranquility of the wicked or even the suffering of the righteous.

In a perfect world, the nice people would prosper, and the evil people would suffer. That is what we think.

Of course, were that the case, everyone would "choose" to be nice simply because it is so obviously advantageous. But it would not be a choice of the nice; it would a choice of the advantages of being nice.

The people who latch on to evil likely think that being evil will bring them greater bounty, less moral responsibility and more fun and material gain.

The perfect world is not so perfect after all. A world in which doing good generates all things good is not a perfect world. A direct link between goodness and prosperity, between evil and poverty, is far from a perfect world, and closer to an artificial world.

But exactly why some people who deserve better continue to suffer, and why some who deserve worse continue to prosper, is beyond our grasp.

Why some marriages that seem so wonderful are fraught with challenges, why some that seem to make no sense continue to thrive, is beyond us.

Frankly, it is not even our business. We are not here to waste time on the whys and the wherefores of others. We are here to do our best, and to leave the rest to God.

❧ MISHNAH 20 ❧

כ. רַבִּי מַתְיָא בֶּן חָרָשׁ אוֹמֵר: הֱוֵי מַקְדִּים בִּשְׁלוֹם כָּל אָדָם, וֶהֱוֵי זָנָב לָאֲרָיוֹת, וְאַל תְּהִי רֹאשׁ לַשׁוּעָלִים.

*Rabbe Matya the son of Harash says: Be the initiator of greetings to all people,
and be a tail among lions rather than a head among foxes.*

When it comes to doing nice things, even simple things like saying hello, do not wait to react. Instead, jump to the fore, specially when it comes to one's life partner.

If each of the partners follows this advice, the partners may fall over each other in the rush to say hello, how are you, or whatever.

Nothing wrong with that.

Additionally, strive for the best, and do not settle for good enough. Lionize your life partner, and thereby let your partner know that your yearning is for the very best for him or her.

❧ MISHNAH 21 ❧

כא. רַבִּי יַעֲקֹב אוֹמֵר: הָעוֹלָם הַזֶּה דּוֹמֶה לִפְרוֹזְדּוֹר בִּפְנֵי הָעוֹלָם הַבָּא.
הַתְקֵן עַצְמְךָ בִּפְרוֹזְדּוֹר כְּדֵי שֶׁתִּכָּנֵס לַטְּרַקְלִין.

*Rabbe Yaakov says: This world is like a vestibule before the world-to-come.
Prepare yourself in the vestibule so that you will be able to enter the banquet
hall.*

This Mishnah adds an extra dimension to marriage. The marriage
partnership extends beyond this world.

The ultimate banquet hall is where the one-ness of marriage as
lived out in this world reaches its full fruition.

It is nice to know that our actions in this world have eternal consequences. It is nice, but also scary. Everything we do counts; every
action, every kindness, every compliment, makes an everlasting
impact.

In this context, when departing from this world, the final word is
not "goodbye." The final words are – "See you later – in the banquet
hall."

How exactly that plays out, specially with having to navigate
second marriages – we leave that to God.

❧ MISHNAH 22 ❧

כב. הוּא הָיָה אוֹמֵר: יָפָה שָׁעָה אַחַת בִּתְשׁוּבָה וּמַעֲשִׂים טוֹבִים בָּעוֹלָם הַזֶּה מִכָּל חַיֵּי הָעוֹלָם הַבָּא, וְיָפָה שָׁעָה אַחַת שֶׁל קוֹרַת רוּחַ בָּעוֹלָם הַבָּא מִכָּל חַיֵּי הָעוֹלָם הַזֶּה.

He [Rabbe Yaakov] used to say: Better is one period of repentance and good deeds in this world than all of life in the world-to-come, and better is one period of spiritual bliss in the world-to-come than all of life in this world.

Following up on the notion of eternality, and how it is an intimidating concept, here Rabbe Yaakov offers a most re-assuring formula.

We are all human; as much as we would like to treat our marital life partner with perfect care and respect, we will probably fall short.

But by working seriously at correcting the shortcomings, by regretting, repenting, and correcting, we reach the height of attainment in this world, so that the bliss of the world-to-come is a realistic eventuality.

What seems intimidating is actually quite inviting. It takes work, but true achievement and fulfillment without working for it was never part of the formula for a meaningful life. Nor should it be.

❧ MISHNAH 23 ❧

כג. רַבִּי שִׁמְעוֹן בֶּן אֶלְעָזָר אוֹמֵר: אַל תְּרַצֶּה אֶת חֲבֵרְךָ בִּשְׁעַת כַּעֲסוֹ,
וְאַל תְּנַחֲמֵהוּ בְּשָׁעָה שֶׁמֵּתוֹ מֻטָּל לְפָנָיו, וְאַל תִּשְׁאַל לוֹ בִּשְׁעַת נִדְרוֹ, וְאַל
תִּשְׁתַּדֵּל לִרְאוֹתוֹ בִּשְׁעַת קַלְקָלָתוֹ.

Rabbe Shimon the son of Elazar says: Do not try to calm your friend at the height of his anger, do not try to comfort your friend when his deceased lies before him, do not question your friend at the time that he makes a vow, and do not seek to see your friend at the time of his humiliation.

There is a normal and understandable instinct to want to help others. Certainly, any caring marital partner will want to help a spouse in travail.

But the key to helping is to weigh most carefully not only the how, but also the when. If the focus is on the other, as it should be, then the time for intervention is not when the intervening spouse wants; it is when the spouse who needs the intervention is receptive to it.

Therefore, the moment of crisis is not usually the time for in-depth conversation. It is the time for tactfully letting your spouse know that you care, and you are with your spouse throughout the crisis, on the ready for further care and conversation whenever it is most appropriate.

❧ MISHNAH 24 ❧

כד. שְׁמוּאֵל הַקָּטָן אוֹמֵר: בִּנְפֹל אוֹיִבְךָ אַל תִּשְׂמָח, וּבִכָּשְׁלוֹ אַל יָגֵל לִבֶּךָ,
פֶּן יִרְאֶה יְיָ וְרַע בְּעֵינָיו, וְהֵשִׁיב מֵעָלָיו אַפּוֹ.

*Shmuel the Younger says: When your enemy falls do not rejoice, and when
your enemy stumbles let not your heart be glad, lest God see this and be
displeased, and turn away the Godly wrath from him* (MISHLAY 24:17–18).

Applied to marriage, this statement might refer to a relationship gone
sour, to the point of divorce.

Not all divorces are amicable. Some are quite bitter, with the couple
previously united in marriage now becoming enemies.

Enmity is a consuming poison. Hard as it may seem, it is best for
both of the divorcing persons to abandon enmity, not to rejoice at the
fall or stumble of one's ex.

Quite the contrary; it is best to hope that one's ex succeeds in
having a better future. Good things usually accrue to those who think
good thoughts.

❧ MISHNAH 25 ❧

כה. אֱלִישָׁע בֶּן אֲבוּיָה אוֹמֵר: הַלּוֹמֵד תּוֹרָה יֶלֶד לְמָה הוּא דוֹמֶה - לִדְיוֹ
כְּתוּבָה עַל נְיָר חָדָשׁ. וְהַלּוֹמֵד תּוֹרָה זָקֵן לְמָה הוּא דוֹמֶה - לִדְיוֹ כְּתוּבָה
עַל נְיָר מָחוּק.

*Elisha the son of Avuya says: One who learns Torah in one's youth, to what
is such a person comparable? To ink written on fresh paper. But one who
learns Torah in one's old age, to what is such a person comparable? To ink
written on used paper.*

Applied to marriage, this Mishnah might be pointing to the advantage
of marrying earlier rather than later.

Obviously, there is a distinct level of maturity that is requisite for
getting married. Maturity is necessary, but not sufficient.

Another necessary ingredient for viable marriage is the willingness
to learn, to adjust from a previous modus operandi to a new reality,
a reality of two instead of one, and all that such adjustment entails;
literally a new way of thinking and behaving.

Learning what it takes for the marriage to thrive is more likely when
one is younger and more able to change; more likely than when one
is older and perhaps more stuck in entrenched habits.

Getting married at any age is possible and desirable, but getting
married when one is more amenable to change has definite merit.

❧ MISHNAH 26 ❧

כו. רַבִּי יוֹסֵי בַּר יְהוּדָה אִישׁ כְּפַר הַבַּבְלִי אוֹמֵר: הַלּוֹמֵד תּוֹרָה מִן הַקְּטַנִּים, לְמָה הוּא דוֹמֶה - לְאוֹכֵל עֲנָבִים קֵהוֹת וְשׁוֹתֶה יַיִן מִגִּתּוֹ. וְהַלּוֹמֵד תּוֹרָה מִן הַזְּקֵנִים, לְמָה הוּא דוֹמֶה - לְאוֹכֵל עֲנָבִים בְּשׁוּלוֹת וְשׁוֹתֶה יַיִן יָשָׁן.

Rabbi Yose the son of Yehuda from Kefar haBavli says: One who learns Torah from the young, to whom is such a person comparable? To one who eats unripe grapes and drinks wine from the press. But one who learns Torah from the old, to whom is such a person comparable? To one who eats ripe grapes and drinks aged wine.

There are advantages to youth, and advantages to older age. It is preferable to learn when one is younger, but at the same time it is preferable to learn from the older, from the wiser; from those who have travelled through life and have absorbed life's lessons.

In truth is it good to learn from anyone, but when it comes to learning what makes marriage work, the sage advice of older people who can speak from first-hand experience is preferable.

❧ MISHNAH 27 ❧

כז. רַבִּי מֵאִיר אוֹמֵר: אַל תִּסְתַּכֵּל בְּקַנְקַן, אֶלָּא בְּמַה שֶׁיֵּשׁ בּוֹ; יֵשׁ קַנְקַן חָדָשׁ מָלֵא יָשָׁן, וְיָשָׁן שֶׁאֲפִילוּ חָדָשׁ אֵין בּוֹ.

Rabbe Meir says: Do not look at the jug, but at what it contains. There could be a new jug with old wine, or an old jug that does not contain even new wine.

When choosing a life partner, externals are understandably enticing, but they might also be misleading.

The key to a person's reality is what resides in the heart. Is it a kind heart or a mean heart? Is it an understanding heart or a hard heart? Is it a warm heart or a cold heart?

It is these less than obvious values that are critical for a flowering relationship.

It is not the bottle, but what resides inside the bottle, that is of highest importance.

❧ MISHNAH 28 ❧

כח. רַבִּי אֶלְעָזָר הַקַּפָּר אוֹמֵר: הַקִּנְאָה וְהַתַּאֲוָה וְהַכָּבוֹד מוֹצִיאִין אֶת הָאָדָם מִן הָעוֹלָם.

Rabbe Elazar haKappar says: Envy, lust, and thirst for honor drive a person out of the world.

The desire, even the need, to have a level of satisfaction with life, is common to most humans.

Having a fulfilling marriage, a partnership of caring and sharing, of giving and receiving, ranks at the very top of attaining satisfaction with life.

Those who are full of envy, lust, and thirst for honor, are arguably less than satisfied with life. They envy because they think they are missing out on something, they lust for a pleasure they think they are lacking, they seek out honor because they feel unrecognized.

In a marriage filled with true love, that is not likely to happen. But when a person's behavior is motivated primarily by the pursuit of narcissistic goals, that behavior drives the person out of the world of meaningful purpose, and on to a path of self-destruction.

❧ MISHNAH 29 ❧

כט. הוּא הָיָה אוֹמֵר: הַיְּלוֹדִים לָמוּת, וְהַמֵּתִים לִחְיוֹת, וְהַחַיִּים לִדּוֹן, לֵידַע
וּלְהוֹדִיעַ וּלְהִוָּדַע שֶׁהוּא אֵל, הוּא הַיּוֹצֵר, הוּא הַבּוֹרֵא, הוּא הַמֵּבִין, הוּא
הַדַּיָּן, הוּא הָעֵד, הוּא בַּעַל דִּין, הוּא עָתִיד לָדּוֹן. בָּרוּךְ הוּא, שֶׁאֵין לְפָנָיו
לֹא עַוְלָה, וְלֹא שִׁכְחָה, וְלֹא מַשּׂוֹא פָנִים, וְלֹא מִקַּח שֹׁחַד, שֶׁהַכֹּל שֶׁלּוֹ.
וְדַע שֶׁהַכֹּל לְפִי הַחֶשְׁבּוֹן; וְאַל יַבְטִיחֲךָ יִצְרָךְ שֶׁהַשְּׁאוֹל בֵּית מָנוֹס לָךְ,
שֶׁעַל כָּרְחֲךָ אַתָּה נוֹצָר, וְעַל כָּרְחֲךָ אַתָּה נוֹלָד, וְעַל כָּרְחֲךָ אַתָּה חַי, וְעַל
כָּרְחֲךָ אַתָּה מֵת, וְעַל כָּרְחֲךָ אַתָּה עָתִיד לִתֵּן דִּין וְחֶשְׁבּוֹן לִפְנֵי מֶלֶךְ מַלְכֵי
הַמְּלָכִים, הַקָּדוֹשׁ בָּרוּךְ הוּא.

*He [Rabbe Elazar haKappar] used to say: Those who are born are destined
to die and those who die are destined to be brought back to life; the living to
be judged – to know, to teach, and to make known that God is Almighty, the
Designer, the Creator, the Discerner, the Judge, the Witness, the Plaintiff,
destined to judge. Blessed is God, before Whom there is no wrong, no forgetfulness, no partiality, and no taking of bribes, for all is God's. Know that all
is according to the reckoning; and let not your impulse convince you that the
grave will be a place of refuge for you, for against your will you are formed,
against your will you are born, against your will do you live, against your
will do you die, and against your will are you destined to give account and
reckoning before the Supreme Ruler of rulers, the Holy One, blessed is God.*

This powerful statement about our destiny speaks volumes about the
essence of life.

We are all here for a purpose. We all have unique strengths and
challenges.

What we do with the gifts and challenges with which we have been
endowed defines how we have succeeded in attaining life's purpose.

This differs from person to person. But we are all better served to
approach life seriously, and not to rely on getting a break when our
life is being judged.

In the marital sphere, it is nice to have an understanding, forgiving
spouse. But to rely on that in advance of doing something that is clearly
wrong is to abuse the blessing that is ours. We preserve the sanctity

of marriage by being strict with ourselves, even demanding, rather than relying on the forgiving generosity of our marriage partner.

The same is true of life, and of our relationship with God. We are here to do our best, not to take short cuts or rely on God's generosity.

This might seem harsh, but in actuality it is a blessing. It is a blessing to know what is expected of us. Such knowledge is most likely to bring out our best throughout our entire life.

Chapter Five

א. בַּעֲשָׂרָה מַאֲמָרוֹת נִבְרָא הָעוֹלָם. וּמַה תַּלְמוּד לוֹמַר, וַהֲלֹא בְּמַאֲמָר
אֶחָד יָכוֹל לְהִבָּרְאוֹת. אֶלָּא לְהִפָּרַע מִן הָרְשָׁעִים שֶׁמְּאַבְּדִין אֶת הָעוֹלָם
שֶׁנִּבְרָא בַּעֲשָׂרָה מַאֲמָרוֹת, וְלִתֵּן שָׂכָר טוֹב לַצַּדִּיקִים שֶׁמְּקַיְּמִין אֶת הָעוֹלָם
שֶׁנִּבְרָא בַּעֲשָׂרָה מַאֲמָרוֹת.

Through ten utterances was the world created. What does this teach us?
Could it not have been created through one utterance? This is in order to
exact penalty from the wicked who destroy the world which was created
through ten utterances, and to give ample reward to the righteous who sustain
the world that was created through ten utterances.

The fact that God created the world with ten utterances, when it
could have been created with one utterance, was to convey how much
importance God ascribed to the world.

Each utterance is an expression of the special significance of each
detail, of the special value of each detail of creation.

Likewise, we exhibit caring for our spouse by being attentive to the
details, that to which our spouse ascribes importance.

❧ MISHNAH 2 ❧

ב. עֲשָׂרָה דוֹרוֹת מֵאָדָם וְעַד נֹחַ, לְהוֹדִיעַ כַּמָּה אֶרֶךְ אַפַּיִם לְפָנָיו, שֶׁכָּל הַדּוֹרוֹת הָיוּ מַכְעִיסִין וּבָאִין, עַד שֶׁהֵבִיא עֲלֵיהֶם אֶת מֵי הַמַּבּוּל.

There were ten generations from Adam to Noah, to make known how long-suffering God is, for all these generations provoked God's anger until God brought the waters of the flood upon them.

This marriage – the marriage between God and the world, ended in divorce; more accurately, the demise of one of the partners.

But it took a long time, and God showed great patience, before realizing that there was no more hope.

Marriage that is facing difficulties cannot wait ten generations, but it is worth having some patience as long as there is a sincere commitment to rectifying, to making matters better.

✣ MISHNAH 3 ✣

ג. עֲשָׂרָה דוֹרוֹת מִנֹּחַ וְעַד אַבְרָהָם, לְהוֹדִיעַ כַּמָּה אֶרֶךְ אַפַּיִם לְפָנָיו, שֶׁכָּל הַדּוֹרוֹת הָיוּ מַכְעִיסִין וּבָאִין, עַד שֶׁבָּא אַבְרָהָם אָבִינוּ וְקִבֵּל שְׂכַר כֻּלָּם.

There were ten generations from Noah to Avraham, to make known how long-suffering God is, for all these generations provoked God's anger until our patriarch Avraham came and received the reward of them all.

The patience in God's second marriage with the world yielded a better result.

Again, it took ten generations of patience, out of which emanated an outstanding, world-saving luminary, our patriarch Avraham.

Patience, and the genuine desire to make amends, to improve, can sometimes give birth to a better marital reality.

❧ MISHNAH 4 ❧

ד. עֲשָׂרָה נִסְיוֹנוֹת נִתְנַסָּה אַבְרָהָם אָבִינוּ, וְעָמַד בְּכֻלָּם, לְהוֹדִיעַ כַּמָּה
חִבָּתוֹ שֶׁל אַבְרָהָם אָבִינוּ.

With ten trials was our patriarch Avraham tested and he stood steadfastly
through all of them, to make known how great was the love of our patriarch
Avraham.

Generally, people prefer to go through life absent any trials and
tribulations.

But realistically, it is impossible to live a full life absent any pain,
or suffering, or tragedy.

When true love exists, and one of the marriage partners is going
through painful times, the other partner feels the pain, and suffers
together with the other.

In true love, nothing gets in between the marriage partners. If
anything, the travail brings them even closer together, as it becomes
so evident how much care and empathy is being shared.

❧ MISHNAH 5 ❧

ה. עֲשָׂרָה נִסִּים נַעֲשׂוּ לַאֲבוֹתֵינוּ בְּמִצְרַיִם, וַעֲשָׂרָה עַל הַיָּם.

Ten miracles were wrought for our ancestors in Egypt, and ten at the sea.

This Mishnah, seemingly just a mere recitation of a fact, serves to highlight a most important feature of our miraculous deliverance from enslavement.

It was a great deliverance, but it was comprised of many significant interventions, each in itself worthy of our attention.

This helps to further increase our gratitude and appreciation, which are so important in our relationship with God, and also with our life marital partner.

❧ MISHNAH 6 ❧

וּ. עֶשֶׂר מַכּוֹת הֵבִיא הַקָּדוֹשׁ בָּרוּךְ הוּא עַל הַמִּצְרִיִּים בְּמִצְרַיִם, וְעֶשֶׂר
עַל הַיָּם.

Ten plagues did the Holy One, blessed is God, bring upon the Egyptians in Egypt, and ten at the sea.

Further to the theme of gratitude, the focus in this Mishnah is on what was visited upon the enemy in order for the Israelites, our ancestors, to be extricated from their travail.

It is another perspective on what it took to attain freedom, an additional host of reasons to be grateful.

Perhaps the lesson here is that we should always look for more reasons to express gratitude. Even if they may seem to be overlapping reasons, as is suggested by the classic commentators, still you cannot say "thank you" too often; you cannot overdose on appreciation.

No matter that the ten miracles wrought for our ancestors were that the plagues visited upon the Egyptians were not visited upon them; that they were protected.

This may amount to saying the same thing twice, just in different terms. The important point is that expressing gratitude in different ways, even for the same thing, is most laudable, in our relationship with God, and in our marital union.

Always look for reasons to be thankful, and then convey that thanks.

✤ MISHNAH 7 ✤

עֲשָׂרָה נִסְיוֹנוֹת נִסּוּ אֲבוֹתֵינוּ אֶת הַקָּדוֹשׁ בָּרוּךְ הוּא בַּמִּדְבָּר, שֶׁנֶּאֱמַר: וַיְנַסּוּ אֹתִי זֶה עֶשֶׂר פְּעָמִים, וְלֹא שָׁמְעוּ בְּקוֹלִי.

Ten times did our fathers test the Holy One, blessed is God, in the wilderness, as it is said – "they have tested Me ten times, and have not listened to My voice" (BEMIDBAR 14:22).

The ten times that our ancestors tested God were certainly all serious breaches, and a far cry from the gratitude that should have defined their actions.

Yet, as provocative as these actions were, and as much harm as they caused to the people, still the people's relationship with God persevered through the crises.

The lesson for marriage is clear – that sometimes we have to steer through turbulent waters so that a meaningful relationship can survive and get back on track.

❧ MISHNAH 8 ❧

ח. עֲשָׂרָה נִסִּים נַעֲשׂוּ לַאֲבוֹתֵינוּ בְּבֵית הַמִּקְדָּשׁ: לֹא הִפִּילָה אִשָּׁה מֵרֵיחַ
בְּשַׂר הַקֹּדֶשׁ, וְלֹא הִסְרִיחַ בְּשַׂר הַקֹּדֶשׁ מֵעוֹלָם, וְלֹא נִרְאָה זְבוּב בְּבֵית
הַמִּטְבָּחַיִם, וְלֹא אֵירַע קֶרִי לְכֹהֵן גָּדוֹל בְּיוֹם הַכִּפּוּרִים, וְלֹא כִבּוּ הַגְּשָׁמִים
אֵשׁ שֶׁל עֲצֵי הַמַּעֲרָכָה, וְלֹא נִצְחָה הָרוּחַ אֶת עַמּוּד הֶעָשָׁן, וְלֹא נִמְצָא
פְּסוּל בָּעוֹמֶר וּבִשְׁתֵּי הַלֶּחֶם וּבְלֶחֶם הַפָּנִים, עוֹמְדִים צְפוּפִים וּמִשְׁתַּחֲוִים
רְוָחִים, וְלֹא הִזִּיק נָחָשׁ וְעַקְרָב בִּירוּשָׁלַיִם, וְלֹא אָמַר אָדָם לַחֲבֵרוֹ: צַר לִי
הַמָּקוֹם שֶׁאָלִין בִּירוּשָׁלָיִם.

Ten miracles were wrought for our ancestors in the Holy Sanctuary: 1) no woman ever miscarried because of the smell of sacred meat; 2) the sacred meat never became putrid; 3) no fly was ever seen in the place the meat was prepared; 4) never did the high priest become unclean on the Day of Atonement; 5) the rain never extinguished the fire of the altar wood-pile; 6) the wind never overcame the smoke column arising from the altar; 7) never was a disqualifying defect found in the omer, the two loaves, or the show breads; 8) the people stood closely pressed together but bowed down with ample room; 9) no snake or scorpion ever inflicted harm in Jerusalem; and 10) no one ever said to a fellow – "The place is too constricted for me that I should lodge in Jerusalem."

These ten are a special breed of miracle. They are miracles not of what happened, such as the splitting of the sea or the falling of the manna, and therefore overt miracles more likely to be recognized.

These are miracles of what did not happen, and therefore more likely to not even be noticed.

Carried into the marital union, it suggests that we include in our gratitude repertoire that of which we may tend to be less aware.

Specific kind actions and expressions that stand out are likely to be noticed, and therefore likely to evoke appropriate reactions.

On the other hand, the absence of undesirable realities might not be picked up.

For example, if the house is generally calm, and the atmosphere is relaxed and free of tension, that is a great blessing, a blessing that takes great effort, and is worthy of expressed gratitude.

In the Holy Sanctuary, we are grateful that meat never spoiled and never caused unwanted consequences, among other things that never happened.

It takes an extra measure of sensitivity to note that which did not occur, and to express gratitude for that. It gives marriage an added dimension of positivity.

✤ MISHNAH 9 ✤

ט. עֲשָׂרָה דְבָרִים נִבְרְאוּ בְּעֶרֶב שַׁבָּת בֵּין הַשְּׁמָשׁוֹת, וְאֵלוּ הֵן: פִּי הָאָרֶץ,
פִּי הַבְּאֵר, פִּי הָאָתוֹן, הַקֶּשֶׁת, וְהַמָּן, וְהַמַּטֶּה, וְהַשָּׁמִיר, הַכְּתָב, וְהַמִּכְתָּב,
וְהַלֻּחוֹת. וְיֵשׁ אוֹמְרִים, אַף הַמַּזִּיקִין, וּקְבוּרָתוֹ שֶׁל מֹשֶׁה רַבֵּינוּ, וְאֵילוֹ שֶׁל
אַבְרָהָם אָבִינוּ. וְיֵשׁ אוֹמְרִים, אַף צְבָת בִּצְבָת עֲשׂוּיָה.

*Ten things were created on the eve of the Shabbos at twilight. They are –
1) the mouth of the earth; 2) the mouth of the well; 3) the mouth of the
donkey; 4) the rainbow; 5) the manna; 6) the rod; 7) the shamir; 8) the
written characters; 9) the writing; and 10) the tablets. Some say also the
destructive demons, the grave of Moshe our teacher, and the ram of our
patriarch Avraham. And others say even the tongs made with tongs.*

Arguably, all these things were items that were not necessary or
essential for creation, such as water, trees, and vegetation, but would
be necessary later on at various points in history.

So, they were created at this point, still in the time of creation, but
at its conclusion, in time for entering the Shabbos with all that the
world needed. Hence, the eve of Shabbos.

The Shabbos is a particularly important time in the marriage, a
time when the daily work pursuits are off limits, and when true human
interaction between the couple is more likely to be uninterrupted by
material matters.

It is of course preferable not to leave preparation for the Shabbos
world till the last minute, but it is highly desirable that all which is
necessary for the Shabbos world be ready, so that the Shabbos can
be meaningfully celebrated by the couple.

❧ MISHNAH 10 ❧

יֹ. שִׁבְעָה דְבָרִים בַּגּוֹלֵם וְשִׁבְעָה בֶּחָכָם. חָכָם אֵינוֹ מְדַבֵּר לִפְנֵי מִי שֶׁגָּדוֹל
מִמֶּנּוּ בְּחָכְמָה וּבְמִנְיָן, וְאֵינוֹ נִכְנָס לְתוֹךְ דִּבְרֵי חֲבֵרוֹ, וְאֵינוֹ נִבְהָל לְהָשִׁיב,
שׁוֹאֵל כָּעִנְיָן וּמֵשִׁיב כַּהֲלָכָה, וְאוֹמֵר עַל רִאשׁוֹן רִאשׁוֹן וְעַל אַחֲרוֹן אַחֲרוֹן,
וְעַל מַה שֶּׁלֹּא שָׁמַע אוֹמֵר לֹא שָׁמַעְתִּי, וּמוֹדֶה עַל הָאֱמֶת; וְחִלּוּפֵיהֶן בַּגּוֹלֵם.

*Seven qualities characterize the boor and seven the wise person. The wise
person 1) does not speak before one who is greater in wisdom and experience;
2) does not break into another person's speaking; 3) is not hasty to answer;
4) questions according to the subject and responds to the point; 5) addresses
first things first and last things last; 6) on what he has not learned he says – "I
have not learned this;" and 7) acknowledges the truth. The reverse of all this
characterizes the boor.*

In the full span of a marriage, there will be reason for the couple to
engage in serious conversation on matters of importance.

Most critical to helpful conversation is adhering to these seven
components; essentially that the couple are attentive to each other,
listen carefully to the views and concerns of the other, and only after
a complete and concentrated listening, then respond carefully and
respectfully.

Letting the other speak without breaking in, thinking before
responding, answering in careful order, and willing to admit to one's
failings, are all essential to assure that the conversation will be helpful.

It boils down to showing respect to the other, both in the way one
listens, and in the way one responds.

❧ MISHNAH 11 ❧

יא. שִׁבְעָה מִינֵי פוּרְעָנִיּוֹת בָּאִין לְעוֹלָם, עַל שִׁבְעָה גוּפֵי עֲבֵרָה. מִקְצָתָן מְעַשְּׂרִין וּמִקְצָתָן אֵינָם מְעַשְּׂרִין, רָעָב שֶׁל מְהוּמָה בָּא, מִקְצָתָן רְעֵבִים וּמִקְצָתָן שְׂבֵעִים. גָּמְרוּ שֶׁלֹּא לְעַשֵּׂר, רָעָב שֶׁל בַּצֹּרֶת בָּא. וְשֶׁלֹּא לִטּוֹל אֶת הַחַלָּה, רָעָב שֶׁל כְּלָיָה בָּא. דֶּבֶר בָּא לְעוֹלָם עַל מִיתוֹת הָאֲמוּרוֹת בַּתּוֹרָה שֶׁלֹּא נִמְסְרוּ לְבֵית דִּין, וְעַל פֵּרוֹת שְׁבִיעִית. חֶרֶב בָּאָה לְעוֹלָם, עַל עִנּוּי הַדִּין, וְעַל עִוּוּת הַדִּין, וְעַל הַמּוֹרִים בַּתּוֹרָה שֶׁלֹּא כַהֲלָכָה. חַיָּה רָעָה בָאָה לְעוֹלָם עַל שְׁבוּעַת שָׁוְא וְעַל חִלּוּל הַשֵּׁם. גָּלוּת בָּא לְעוֹלָם עַל עֲבוֹדָה זָרָה, וְעַל גִּלּוּי עֲרָיוֹת, וְעַל שְׁפִיכוּת דָּמִים, וְעַל שְׁמִטַּת הָאָרֶץ.

Seven forms of calamity come upon the world for seven types of transgression. 1) If some tithe and others do not, famine from drought ensues, some suffer hunger while some are satisfied; 2) if all decide not to tithe, famine through panic and drought ensues; 3) if all decide not to set aside the dough offering, an all-consuming famine ensues; 4) pestilence comes upon the world for the commission of those capital crimes enumerated in the Torah, the punishments for which were not turned over to a human court, and for violations of the law concerning produce of the sabbatical year; 5) the sword comes upon the world for the delay of justice, for the distortion of justice, and for those who render Torah law perversely; 6) wild beasts come upon the world because of vain swearing and the desecration of God's Name; 7) exile comes upon the world because of idolatry, immorality, murder, and violation of the law for resting the soil in the sabbatical year.

The Mishnah here shares the cause-and-effect nature of our actions. It is built-in to the way of the world that failure to live up to responsibilities leads to adverse consequences.

Though it is always nice to have a forgiving spouse, it is not nice to rely on that nice understanding and consequently not live up to the responsibilities that are fundamental to marriage.

It is to be expected that failure to live up to one's obligations will impact negatively on the relationship.

❧ MISHNAH 12 ❧

יב. בְּאַרְבָּעָה פְרָקִים הַדֶּבֶר מִתְרַבֶּה - בָּרְבִיעִית, וּבַשְּׁבִיעִית, וּבְמוֹצָאֵי שְׁבִיעִית, וּבְמוֹצָאֵי הֶחָג שֶׁבְּכָל שָׁנָה וְשָׁנָה. בָּרְבִיעִית, מִפְּנֵי מַעֲשַׂר עָנִי שֶׁבַּשְּׁלִישִׁית; בַּשְּׁבִיעִית, מִפְּנֵי מַעֲשַׂר עָנִי שֶׁבַּשִּׁשִּׁית; בְּמוֹצָאֵי שְׁבִיעִית, מִפְּנֵי פֵּרוֹת שְׁבִיעִית; בְּמוֹצָאֵי הֶחָג שֶׁבְּכָל שָׁנָה וְשָׁנָה, מִפְּנֵי גֶזֶל מַתְּנוֹת עֲנִיִּים.

During four periods pestilence proliferates – in the fourth year, in the seventh year, at the conclusion of the seventh year, and at the conclusion of the Tabernacles feast every year. In the fourth year for neglecting the tithe for the poor in the third year; in the seventh year for neglecting the tithe for the poor in the sixth year; at the conclusion of the seventh year for neglecting the law concerning produce of the sabbatical year; at the conclusion of the Tabernacles feast every year for robbing the poor of their prescribed gifts.

There are specific times of the year that are more vulnerable to the consequences of neglect.

In marriage, there are likewise times of the year that call for special attentiveness, be it birthdays or celebrative times, or commemorations of untimely events.

Here too, being careful, caring, attentive, and appropriate to the occasion is highly recommended.

✤ MISHNAH 13 ✤

יג. אַרְבַּע מִדּוֹת בָּאָדָם: הָאוֹמֵר שֶׁלִּי שֶׁלִּי וְשֶׁלְּךָ שֶׁלָּךְ, זוֹ מִדָּה בֵּינוֹנִית;
וְיֵשׁ אוֹמְרִים, זוֹ מִדַּת סְדוֹם. שֶׁלִּי שֶׁלְּךָ וְשֶׁלְּךָ שֶׁלִּי, עַם הָאָרֶץ. שֶׁלִּי שֶׁלְּךָ
וְשֶׁלְּךָ שֶׁלָּךְ, חָסִיד. שֶׁלִּי שֶׁלִּי וְשֶׁלְּךָ שֶׁלִּי, רָשָׁע.

There are four character types among people. One who says – "what is mine is mine and what is yours is yours" is of average character, and others say this is the characteristic of Sedom; one who says – "what is mine is yours and what is yours is mine" is an ignoramus; one who says – "what is mine is yours and what is yours is yours" is a pious person; one who says – "what is yours is mine and what is mine is mine" is an evil person.

One can easily see how this characterization of different sharing types applies to marriage.

A one-sided, "everything is mine" ownership pattern is clearly a recipe for disaster.

On the other hand, a much better other hand at that, a one-sided "everything is yours" ownership pattern is such a welcome escalation of marital harmony.

Even the seemingly neutral approach, which looks average, i.e., "what is mine is mine and what is yours is yours," can easily disintegrate into Sedom-like nastiness if it becomes a strictly enforced rule in the house.

In this and so many other life interactions, the more one gives, the more one receives.

✤ MISHNAH 14 ✤

יד. אַרְבַּע מִדּוֹת בַּדֵּעוֹת: נוֹחַ לִכְעוֹס וְנוֹחַ לִרְצוֹת, יָצָא הֶפְסֵדוֹ בִּשְׂכָרוֹ;
קָשֶׁה לִכְעוֹס וְקָשֶׁה לִרְצוֹת, יָצָא שְׂכָרוֹ בְּהֶפְסֵדוֹ; קָשֶׁה לִכְעוֹס וְנוֹחַ לִרְצוֹת,
חָסִיד; נוֹחַ לִכְעוֹס וְקָשֶׁה לִרְצוֹת, רָשָׁע.

*There are four types of disposition. Easy to provoke and easy to pacify – the
loss disappears in that person's gain; difficult to provoke and difficult to
pacify – the gain disappears in that person's loss; difficult to provoke and easy
to pacify – this characterizes the pious person; easy to provoke and difficult
to pacify – this characterizes the evil person.*

Anger anywhere is unwelcome. Anger in the home is a consuming
poison.

Obviously, the best alternative is to never get angry. The variations
offered here work with the presumption that we are all capable of
becoming angry.

Realistically, if nothing in life causes us to become angry, that
indicates that we lack passion; that we have a caring deficiency.

The anger referred to here seems to address relationship-related
anger. To be provoked and to be pacified are terms that relate to
personal dealings.

If the anger is because of injustice, a more legitimate anger, then
the anger should abate only if the injustice is removed or corrected.

In the marriage realm, the prevailing love between the spouses
should ideally prevent any anger from erupting. But if anger does
erupt, it should quickly dissipate because of that love.

❧ MISHNAH 15 ❧

טו. אַרְבַּע מִדּוֹת בְּתַלְמִידִים: מַהֵר לִשְׁמֹעַ וּמַהֵר לְאַבֵּד, יָצָא שְׂכָרוֹ
בְּהֶפְסֵדוֹ; קָשֶׁה לִשְׁמֹעַ וְקָשֶׁה לְאַבֵּד, יָצָא הֶפְסֵדוֹ בִּשְׂכָרוֹ; מַהֵר לִשְׁמֹעַ
וְקָשֶׁה לְאַבֵּד, זֶה חֵלֶק טוֹב; קָשֶׁה לִשְׁמֹעַ וּמַהֵר לְאַבֵּד, זֶה חֵלֶק רָע.

*There are four types among students. Quick to learn and quick to forget –
the gain disappears in that person's loss; slow to understand and slow to
forget – the loss disappears in that person's gain; quick to learn and slow to
forget – that is a good portion; slow to learn and quick to forget – that is a
bad portion.*

It is quite clear what is the best choice, namely to be quick to learn and
slow to forget. Even better would it be never to forget.

At the same time, it is most helpful to see ourselves as students,
always ready and eager to learn, and thereby to improve.

Marriage too is a learning endeavor, in which we always learn more
about our marriage partner, and more about how to be a superior
marriage partner.

That is the good portion, for both of the marriage partners.

✦ MISHNAH 16 ✦

טז. אַרְבַּע מִדּוֹת בְּנוֹתְנֵי צְדָקָה: הָרוֹצֶה שֶׁיִּתֵּן וְלֹא יִתְּנוּ אֲחֵרִים, עֵינוֹ רָעָה בְּשֶׁל אֲחֵרִים; יִתְּנוּ אֲחֵרִים וְהוּא לֹא יִתֵּן, עֵינוֹ רָעָה בְּשֶׁלּוֹ; יִתֵּן וְיִתְּנוּ אֲחֵרִים, חָסִיד; לֹא יִתֵּן וְלֹא יִתְּנוּ אֲחֵרִים, רָשָׁע.

There are four types among givers of charity. One who desires to give but that others should not give begrudges what belongs to others; one who desires that others should give but he not give begrudges what belongs to himself; one who desires to give and that others should give is pious; one who does not desire to give and that others should not give is evil.

Piety regarding charity inheres in our desire to give, combined with an equal desire that others should give.

Translated more generally, it suggests that our desire to do good should be combined with a desire that others should likewise do the same.

Wanting to do good but wanting others to behave in a contrary fashion reduces our own expression of the good to a mean-spirited, narcissistic expression. If good is good, it is good for everyone.

Wanting our marital partner to excel should be a most natural and welcome component of the marriage compact.

❧ MISHNAH 17 ❧

יז. אַרְבַּע מִדּוֹת בְּהוֹלְכֵי בֵית הַמִּדְרָשׁ: הוֹלֵךְ וְאֵינוֹ עוֹשֶׂה, שְׂכַר הֲלִיכָה
בְּיָדוֹ; עוֹשֶׂה וְאֵינוֹ הוֹלֵךְ, שְׂכַר מַעֲשֶׂה בְּיָדוֹ; הוֹלֵךְ וְעוֹשֶׂה, חָסִיד; לֹא הוֹלֵךְ
וְלֹא עוֹשֶׂה, רָשָׁע.

There are four types among those who attend the house of study. One who
goes but does not practice secures the reward for going; one who practices but
does not go secures the reward for practicing; one who attends and practices
is pious; one who neither attends nor practices is evil.

The commitment to excel is appropriate not only by each of the marital
partners for the other; i.e., that the other should excel in all ways.

It is similarly appropriate that each of the partners sustain an
unyielding desire to be better today than yesterday, and better tomorrow than today.

One very welcome way to achieve regular improvement is by study;
to learn more, to know more, and thereby to implement better.

Piety, being serious and dedicated to living life in the most responsible manner, is achieved by the dedication to learning that is then
put into practice.

So, for example, it is most essential to learn what are the full
parameters of responsible speech; speech that avoids even a tinge of
slander or evil talk, speech that is full of respectfulness and caring.

The couple who learn this, and then implement this in their home,
thereby manifest a most profound level of piety.

✿ MISHNAH 18 ✿

יח. אַרְבַּע מִדּוֹת בְּיוֹשְׁבִים לִפְנֵי חֲכָמִים: סְפוֹג, וּמַשְׁפֵּךְ, מְשַׁמֶּרֶת, וְנָפָה.
סְפוֹג, שֶׁהוּא סוֹפֵג אֶת הַכֹּל; וּמַשְׁפֵּךְ, שֶׁמַּכְנִיס בְּזוֹ וּמוֹצִיא בְּזוֹ; מְשַׁמֶּרֶת,
שֶׁמּוֹצִיאָה אֶת הַיַּיִן וְקוֹלֶטֶת אֶת הַשְּׁמָרִים; וְנָפָה, שֶׁמּוֹצִיאָה אֶת הַקֶּמַח
וְקוֹלֶטֶת אֶת הַסֹּלֶת.

There are four types among those who sit before the sages – the sponge, the funnel, the strainer, and the sieve. The sponge, because it absorbs everything; the funnel, because it lets in at one end and out at the other; the strainer, because it lets the wine out and retains the sediment; and the sieve, because it lets out the bran and retains the fine flour.

The desire to learn, in order to know, and then to be able to implement, is truly laudable.

But the rush to this noble endeavor is best achieved through careful listening.

The couple who do this in order to enhance the marriage, be it before or during the marriage, should engage in judicious listening, so that they absorb carefully and apply lovingly, with full appreciation of the hierarchy of importance.

It is therefore vital to retain the flour, in order for the marriage to flower.

❧ MISHNAH 19 ❧

יט. כָּל אַהֲבָה שֶׁהִיא תְלוּיָה בְדָבָר, בָּטֵל דָּבָר בְּטֵלָה אַהֲבָה; וְשֶׁאֵינָה תְלוּיָה בְדָבָר, אֵינָה בְּטֵלָה לְעוֹלָם. אֵיזוֹ הִיא אַהֲבָה שֶׁהִיא תְלוּיָה בְדָבָר, זוֹ אַהֲבַת אַמְנוֹן וְתָמָר; וְשֶׁאֵינָה תְלוּיָה בְדָבָר, זוֹ אַהֲבַת דָּוִד וִיהוֹנָתָן.

Any love which is contingent on a tangible thing, when the thing is nullified the love disintegrates; but a love which is not contingent on a tangible thing will never disintegrate. What is the prototype of a contingent love? That is the love of Amnon and Tamar. And what is the prototype of a love which is not contingent on any tangible thing? That is the love of David and Yonatan.

Love which is contingent on a tangible thing is verily not true love. Because it is not true love, sooner or later it will collapse.

There are relationships that seem to be based on "things," material realities, that appear to last, in apparent contradiction of this somewhat categorical Mishnah statement.

It is probably not a good idea to delve into the details of other peoples' relationships. There may be more to the relationships than we know.

Additionally, and this is a most crucial point, it is entirely possible for a relationship to begin on the wrong footing, based on externals that do not last forever.

However, that skewered relationship, which began with the wrong priorities, might actually develop, such that the couple grow beyond the original reasons for marrying, and develop a truly meaningful and unconditional connection.

It is called maturing, achieved by growing through learning, listening, appreciating, gaining a more encompassing perspective on life in general, and on each other in particular.

This is the type of love for which the couple should strive. Ideally, it should be the basis for the union in the first place. But failing that, there still remains every opportunity for the couple to attain that level of love.

In a word, this Mishnah is teaching us that we should choose a marriage partner not based on what the other *has*, but on who the other *is*.

❧ MISHNAH 20 ❧

כ. כָּל מַחֲלֹוקֶת שֶׁהִיא לְשֵׁם שָׁמַיִם, סוֹפָהּ לְהִתְקַיֵּם, וְשֶׁאֵינָהּ לְשֵׁם שָׁמַיִם,
אֵין סוֹפָהּ לְהִתְקַיֵּם. אֵיזוֹ הִיא מַחֲלֹוקֶת שֶׁהִיא לְשֵׁם שָׁמַיִם, זוֹ מַחֲלֹוקֶת
הִלֵּל וְשַׁמַּאי. וְשֶׁאֵינָהּ לְשֵׁם שָׁמַיִם, זוֹ מַחֲלֹוקֶת קֹרַח וְכָל עֲדָתוֹ.

*Every controversy which is for the sake of Heaven will ultimately endure,
but one that is not for the sake of Heaven will ultimately not endure. What
is the prototype of a controversy that is for the sake of Heaven? This is the
controversy between Hillel and Shammai. And what is the prototype for
one that is not for the sake of Heaven? This is the controversy of Korah
and all his cohorts.*

Marital bliss, marital harmony, does not preclude the couple having
differences of opinion.

As long as the couple share common goals, the differences on
how to attain those goals, however serious they may be, will likely
be resolved not merely amicably, but with genuine mutual appreciation.

Arguments about silly, material matters fall far short of being
arguments for the sake of Heaven.

It is important for each of the marital partners to be honest with
themselves, to think carefully about whether this or that matter is
worth having an argument.

And then, having passed this most vital test, it is then critically
important that the ensuing conversation does not disintegrate into a
clash of egos, and is instead sharply focused on what is truly best for
the couple, and the family of the couple.

This type of discussion is likely to lead to enduring outcomes.

❧ MISHNAH 21 ❧

כא. כָּל הַמְזַכֶּה אֶת הָרַבִּים, אֵין חֵטְא בָּא עַל יָדוֹ; וְכָל הַמַּחֲטִיא אֶת
הָרַבִּים, אֵין מַסְפִּיקִין בְּיָדוֹ לַעֲשׂוֹת תְּשׁוּבָה. מֹשֶׁה זָכָה וְזִכָּה אֶת הָרַבִּים,
זְכוּת הָרַבִּים תָּלוּי בּוֹ, שֶׁנֶּאֱמַר: צִדְקַת יְיָ עָשָׂה, וּמִשְׁפָּטָיו עִם יִשְׂרָאֵל.
יָרָבְעָם בֶּן נְבָט חָטָא וְהֶחֱטִיא אֶת הָרַבִּים, חֵטְא הָרַבִּים תָּלוּי בּוֹ, שֶׁנֶּאֱמַר:
עַל חַטֹּאות יָרָבְעָם אֲשֶׁר חָטָא, וַאֲשֶׁר הֶחֱטִיא אֶת יִשְׂרָאֵל.

*Whoever causes the multitude to be virtuous, no sin shall come through
that person; but one who causes the multitude to sin will not be given the
opportunity to repent. Moshe was himself virtuous and caused the multitude
to be virtuous, therefore the virtue of the multitude is ascribed to him, as it
is written – "he performed the righteousness of God and God's judgments
with Israel" (DEVARIM 33:21). Yeravam the son of Nevat sinned and caused
the multitude to sin, therefore the sin of the multitude is ascribed to him, as
it is written – "For the sins of Yeravam which he sinned and wherewith he
caused Israel to sin . . ." (I MELAKHIM 15:30).*

Each of the partners in a marriage has a unique ability to exert influ-
ence on the other, be it consciously or unconsciously.

One who is virtuous, who has the right values, and who lives those
values, will almost automatically inspire and uplift the other.

On the other hand, one whose values are deficient, and whose
behavior is lacking, will generate a negative atmosphere with unwelcome repercussions.

Thus, one who is kind, gracious, appreciative, cooperative, and full
of gratitude, is likely to evoke such reaction in the marital partner.

But one who is mean, nasty, ungrateful, and dour will create an
atmosphere in which these negative and destructive patterns perpetuate.

It is self-evident which is the preferred choice. At the same time,
it is imperative that each of the marital partners embrace this choice
on their own, rather than placing the onus for proper interaction on
the other.

The Hebrew word for marriage, *nisuin*, literally refers to uplifting.
Uplifting each other is marriage at its best.

❧

❧ MISHNAH 22 ❧

כב. כָּל מִי שֶׁיֵּשׁ בְּיָדוֹ שְׁלֹשָׁה דְבָרִים הַלָּלוּ, מִתַּלְמִידָיו שֶׁל אַבְרָהָם אָבִינוּ;
וּשְׁלֹשָׁה דְבָרִים אֲחֵרִים, מִתַּלְמִידָיו שֶׁל בִּלְעָם הָרָשָׁע. עַיִן טוֹבָה, וְרוּחַ
נְמוּכָה, וְנֶפֶשׁ שְׁפָלָה, מִתַּלְמִידָיו שֶׁל אַבְרָהָם אָבִינוּ. עַיִן רָעָה, וְרוּחַ גְּבוֹהָה,
וְנֶפֶשׁ רְחָבָה, מִתַּלְמִידָיו שֶׁל בִּלְעָם הָרָשָׁע. מַה בֵּין תַּלְמִידָיו שֶׁל אַבְרָהָם
אָבִינוּ לְתַלְמִידָיו שֶׁל בִּלְעָם הָרָשָׁע. תַּלְמִידָיו שֶׁל אַבְרָהָם אָבִינוּ אוֹכְלִין
בָּעוֹלָם הַזֶּה וְנוֹחֲלִין בָּעוֹלָם הַבָּא, שֶׁנֶּאֱמַר: לְהַנְחִיל אֹהֲבַי יֵשׁ, וְאֹצְרֹתֵיהֶם
אֲמַלֵּא. אֲבָל תַּלְמִידָיו שֶׁל בִּלְעָם הָרָשָׁע יוֹרְשִׁין גֵּיהִנֹּם וְיוֹרְדִין לִבְאֵר שַׁחַת,
שֶׁנֶּאֱמַר: וְאַתָּה אֱלֹהִים תּוֹרִידֵם לִבְאֵר שַׁחַת, אַנְשֵׁי דָמִים וּמִרְמָה לֹא יֶחֱצוּ
יְמֵיהֶם, וַאֲנִי אֶבְטַח בָּךְ.

Anyone who possesses these three traits is among the disciples of our patriarch Avraham, but anyone who possesses three other traits is among the disciples of the evil Bil'am. A good eye, a humble spirit, and a contented soul are the traits of the disciples of our patriarch Avraham; a bad eye, an arrogant spirit, and an insatiable soul are the traits of the disciples of the evil Bil'am. What is the difference between the disciples of our patriarch Avraham and the disciples of the evil Bil'am? The disciples of our patriarch Avraham are sustained in this world and inherit the world-to-come, as it is said – "To those who love Me I have what to bequeath, and I shall fill their treasure houses" (MISHLAY 8:21). But the disciples of the evil Bil'am inherit Gehinnom and descend into the pit of destruction, as it is said – "But you, God, will bring them down into the pit of destruction, people of blood and deceit shall not live out half their days, but I will trust in You" (TEHILLIM 55:24).

The choice between being a disciple of our patriarch Avraham or a disciple of Bil'am is a choice between good and evil; not really a choice.

But more precisely, what is it about our patriarch Avraham that we should rush to embrace?

One with a *good eye* rejoices in the good that is achieved by others, and is happy rather than envious at their success.

A *humble spirit* refers to those who do great things, but do not think that because of those achievements they are better than others, and deserve superior treatment.

Finally, a *contented soul* is satisfied with life, appreciating the blessings and not lamenting or pursuing what is lacking.

These three virtues, present in abundance in our patriarch Avraham, are wonderful virtues that beautify a marriage. Rejoicing in the good realized by one's spouse, always being humble and gentle, and being content and happy, almost guarantee that the marriage is of the extraordinary type.

❧ MISHNAH 23 ❧

כג. יְהוּדָה בֶּן תֵּימָא אוֹמֵר: הֱוֵי עַז כַּנָּמֵר, וְקַל כַּנֶּשֶׁר, רָץ כַּצְּבִי, וְגִבּוֹר כָּאֲרִי, לַעֲשׂוֹת רְצוֹן אָבִיךָ שֶׁבַּשָּׁמָיִם.

Yehuda the son of Tayma says: Be strong as a leopard, light as an eagle, swift as a gazelle, and mighty as a lion, to do the will of your Father in heaven.

A strong relationship is an energizing relationship. Love of God brings with it a strong desire to fulfill God's will. Nothing can hold the believer from actualizing God's commands.

In a true loving marriage, each of the couple, without being asked, cannot be held back from doing whatever it takes to make the other happy, to help realize the other's will.

❧ MISHNAH 24 ❧

כד. הוּא הָיָה אוֹמֵר: עַז פָּנִים לְגֵיהִנֹּם, וּבוֹשֶׁת פָּנִים לְגַן עֵדֶן. יְהִי רָצוֹן
מִלְּפָנֶיךָ, יְיָ אֱלֹהֵינוּ וֵאלֹהֵי אֲבוֹתֵינוּ, שֶׁיִּבָּנֶה בֵּית הַמִּקְדָּשׁ בִּמְהֵרָה בְיָמֵינוּ,
וְתֵן חֶלְקֵנוּ בְּתוֹרָתֶךָ.

*He [Yehuda the son of Tayma] used to say: The arrogant person is headed
for Gehinnom, and the shamefaced individual is headed for the Garden of
Eden. May it be Your will, Lord our God, that the Holy Sanctuary be rebuilt
speedily in our days and grant us our portion in Your Torah.*

As resolute as one must be to fulfill one's obligations with all the
strength one can muster, it can become dangerous if the strength one
exhibits is of the get-out-of-my-way type.

The bully-like approach in which one leaps into life almost oblivious to everyone else, and likely causes much harm on the way, is not
the desired approach.

Instead, treading delicately, shamefacedly, with great caution, so as
to not harm anyone on the way, is the preferred approach.

Within marriage, the uncontrolled, overpowering, head-first
leap into fulfilling one's obligations will most likely lead to abusive
behavior.

We are asked to fulfill our obligations with a delicate balance of
personal responsibility and consideration for others; to do things in
the right balance so that in our yearning to achieve, we do not inflict
harm.

This is indeed a most challenging directive, as there are so many
potential obstacles to achieving this balance.

We conclude with the fervent hope that the Holy Sanctuary will be
rebuilt, and the ambience of that holiness will help everyone achieve
that balance in profound spiritual sensitivity.

✤ MISHNAH 25 ✤

כה. הוּא הָיָה אוֹמֵר: בֶּן חָמֵשׁ שָׁנִים לַמִּקְרָא, בֶּן עֶשֶׂר שָׁנִים לַמִּשְׁנָה, בֶּן
שְׁלֹשׁ עֶשְׂרֵה לַמִּצְוֹת, בֶּן חֲמֵשׁ עֶשְׂרֵה לַגְּמָרָא, בֶּן שְׁמוֹנֶה עֶשְׂרֵה לַחֻפָּה, בֶּן
עֶשְׂרִים לִרְדּוֹף, בֶּן שְׁלֹשִׁים לַכֹּחַ, בֶּן אַרְבָּעִים לַבִּינָה, בֶּן חֲמִשִּׁים לָעֵצָה, בֶּן
שִׁשִּׁים לְזִקְנָה, בֶּן שִׁבְעִים לְשֵׂיבָה, בֶּן שְׁמוֹנִים לַגְּבוּרָה, בֶּן תִּשְׁעִים לָשׁוּחַ,
בֶּן מֵאָה כְּאִלּוּ מֵת וְעָבַר וּבָטֵל מִן הָעוֹלָם.

*He [Yehuda the son of Tayma] used to say: Five years is the age of readiness
for the study of Scripture; ten years for the study of Mishnah; thirteen years
for fulfilling the precepts; fifteen years for the study of the Talmud; eighteen
years for marriage; twenty years for pursuit of a livelihood; thirty years for
strength; forty years for understanding; fifty years for counsel; sixty years
for old age; seventy years for fullness of years; eighty years for might; ninety
years for being bent; one hundred years for being as if already dead and
having passed away from the world.*

The guidelines herein proposed offer the general parameters for
attaining a responsible life balance. It can perhaps serve as an antidote
to ward off the impatience turned into arrogance that Rabbe Yehuda
warned against in the previous Mishnah.

If we place centrality on marriage within these stages of develop-
ment, the Mishnah divides into three stages.

The first stage is the preparatory stage, the stage of study, learning
about the fullness of one's responsibility.

The second stage is sharing that learned responsibility with one's
life partner.

The third stage, the stage following marriage, involves embarking
on life together in full awareness of life's usual trajectory.

This could be seen as the contours of a life game-plan, the general
guideposts within which life unfolds.

With this general framework, serving as the parameters within
which the couple blend together toward realizing their joint destiny,
the couple are provided with the vital insights on how their life
together reaches fruition.

❧ MISHNAH 26 ☙

כו. בֶּן בַּג בַּג אוֹמֵר: הֲפָךְ בָּהּ וַהֲפָךְ בָּהּ, דְּכֹלָּא בָהּ, וּבָהּ תֶּחֱזֵי, וְסִיב וּבְלֵה בָהּ, וּמִנָּהּ לָא תָזוּעַ, שֶׁאֵין לָךְ מִדָּה טוֹבָה הֵימֶנָּה.

The son of Bag Bag says: Turn it and turn it for all is in it and through it you will perceive clearly; grow old and gray in it and from it do not depart, for there is no better virtue for you than it.

This exhortation addresses the matter of fidelity to the Torah. The Torah in its enveloping fullness addresses the totality of life, from beginning to end.

The direction it offers covers life in its entirety. Even if some nuances may be lost on us, it is only because we have not given the Torah proper attention.

Fidelity to one's spouse likewise carries with it the sacred obligation to see the marriage as embracing the fullness of life.

This means seeing one's fulfillment within the context of marital togetherness, including the stage wherein we *grow old and gray.*

❧ MISHNAH 27 ❧

כז. בֶּן הֵא הֵא אוֹמֵר: לְפוּם צַעֲרָא אַגְרָא.

The son of Hae Hae says: According to the exertion is the reward.

This formula works with so many components of life. What we get out of life is commensurate with what we put in.

If we apply ourselves whole-heartedly, diligently, responsibly, caringly, lovingly, and genuinely to our marriage, this will be reflected in the reward of a meaningful, blissful, harmonious, and fulfilling union.

Chapter Six

שָׁנוּ חֲכָמִים בִּלְשׁוֹן הַמִּשְׁנָה – בָּרוּךְ שֶׁבָּחַר בָּהֶם וּבְמִשְׁנָתָם.

The sages taught in in the language of the Mishnah – Source of all blessing is God, Who chose them and their teaching.

This chapter is not comprised of Mishnah statements, as redacted by Rabbe Yehuda haNasi. They are contemporaneous with the redaction, but are known as beraita, statements of the sages of that period but taught outside the study hall of Rabbe Yehuda haNasi.

They are taught in the same language as the Mishnah, and like Mishnah expand on the Torah to apply the Torah to all circumstance, including, for our purposes, marriage.

We express here our acknowledgement of God as the Source of all blessing. That blessing includes choosing the sages who expound on God's word and apply it to the fullness of life, marriage included.

❧ MISHNAH 1 ❧

א. רַבִּי מֵאִיר אוֹמֵר: כָּל הָעוֹסֵק בַּתּוֹרָה לִשְׁמָהּ זוֹכֶה לִדְבָרִים הַרְבֵּה, וְלֹא
עוֹד, אֶלָּא שֶׁכָּל הָעוֹלָם כֻּלּוֹ כְּדַאי הוּא לוֹ. נִקְרָא רֵעַ, אָהוּב, אוֹהֵב אֶת
הַמָּקוֹם, אוֹהֵב אֶת הַבְּרִיּוֹת, מְשַׂמֵּחַ אֶת הַמָּקוֹם, מְשַׂמֵּחַ אֶת הַבְּרִיּוֹת.
וּמַלְבַּשְׁתּוֹ עֲנָוָה וְיִרְאָה, וּמַכְשַׁרְתּוֹ לִהְיוֹת צַדִּיק, חָסִיד, יָשָׁר, וְנֶאֱמָן,
וּמְרַחַקְתּוֹ מִן הַחֵטְא, וּמְקָרַבְתּוֹ לִידֵי זְכוּת. וְנֶהֱנִין מִמֶּנּוּ עֵצָה וְתוּשִׁיָּה,
בִּינָה וּגְבוּרָה, שֶׁנֶּאֱמַר: לִי עֵצָה וְתוּשִׁיָּה, אֲנִי בִינָה, לִי גְבוּרָה. וְנוֹתֶנֶת לוֹ
מַלְכוּת וּמֶמְשָׁלָה, וְחִקּוּר דִּין, וּמְגַלִּין לוֹ רָזֵי תוֹרָה, וְנַעֲשֶׂה כְּמַעְיָן הַמִּתְגַּבֵּר
וּכְנָהָר שֶׁאֵינוֹ פוֹסֵק, וְהֹוֶה צָנוּעַ, וְאֶרֶךְ רוּחַ, וּמוֹחֵל עַל עֶלְבּוֹנוֹ. וּמְגַדַּלְתּוֹ
וּמְרוֹמַמְתּוֹ עַל כָּל הַמַּעֲשִׂים.

*Rabbe Meir says: Whoever occupies one's self with Torah for its own sake
merits many things; moreover, such a person is sufficient reason for the
continued existence of the entire world. Such a person is called friend, beloved,
lover of God, lover of humankind, a bringer of joy to God, a bringer of joy
to humankind. The Torah clothes such a person in humility and awe and
enables that person to be righteous, pious, upright and faithful; the Torah
keeps that person far from sin and brings that person to virtue. Through
such a person people benefit in terms of counsel and sound wisdom, as it is
said – "Counsel is mine and sound wisdom; I am understanding, strength is
mine" (MISHLAY 8:14). It gives such a person sovereignty, dominion and
discerning judgment; the secrets of the Torah are revealed to that person, who
becomes like a spring that never fails and a river which gains in strength, and
remains modest, patient, and forgiving of insults. The Torah magnifies and
exalts that person over all creatures.*

This entire chapter is dedicated to acquiring Torah, and is often
referred to by that name, *Kinyan Torah.*

For our purposes, we focus on the Torah for marriage, with this
last chapter serving as the punctuating climactic appreciation of Torah
wisdom as so essential to marriage.

This statement of Rabbe Meir, extolling those who embrace Torah
for its own sake, not for fame or gain, applies so aptly to those who
marry not for what they will gain, but for what they will give.

True, when one gives, one is more likely to receive, but when the true intention is to convey loving affection in a most respectful and caring manner, because that is the Torah prescription for marriage, such intent justifies existence.

Such a person brings joy to God and to one's spouse. Moreover, through generating meaningful joy one uplifts humanity.

The embrace of marriage in its full profundity brings with it a complete host of values, including humility, righteousness, and piety.

Such a couple is truly exalted in so many ways.

❧ MISHNAH 2 ❧

ב. אָמַר רַבִּי יְהוֹשֻׁעַ בֶּן לֵוִי: בְּכָל יוֹם וָיוֹם בַּת קוֹל יוֹצֵאת מֵהַר חוֹרֵב וּמַכְרֶזֶת
וְאוֹמֶרֶת - אוֹי לָהֶם לַבְּרִיּוֹת מֵעֶלְבּוֹנָהּ שֶׁל תּוֹרָה, שֶׁכָּל מִי שֶׁאֵינוֹ עוֹסֵק
בַּתּוֹרָה נִקְרָא נָזוּף, שֶׁנֶּאֱמַר: נֶזֶם זָהָב בְּאַף חֲזִיר, אִשָּׁה יָפָה וְסָרַת טָעַם.
וְאוֹמֵר: וְהַלֻּחֹת מַעֲשֵׂה אֱלֹהִים הֵמָּה וְהַמִּכְתָּב מִכְתַּב אֱלֹהִים הוּא, חָרוּת
עַל הַלֻּחֹת - אַל תִּקְרֵי חָרוּת אֶלָּא חֵרוּת, שֶׁאֵין לְךָ בֶּן חוֹרִין, אֶלָּא מִי
שֶׁעוֹסֵק בְּתַלְמוּד תּוֹרָה. וְכָל מִי שֶׁעוֹסֵק בְּתַלְמוּד תּוֹרָה, הֲרֵי זֶה מִתְעַלֶּה,
שֶׁנֶּאֱמַר: וּמִמַּתָּנָה נַחֲלִיאֵל, וּמִנַּחֲלִיאֵל בָּמוֹת.

Rabbe Yehoshua the son of Levi says: Day after day a heavenly voice issues
from Mount Horeb proclaiming the following – "Woe to humankind for
their contempt of the Torah," for whoever is not occupied with the Torah is
considered rebuked, as it is said – "As a golden ring in a swine's snout, so is
*a beautiful woman who deviates from discretion" (*MISHLAY 11:22*). And*
scripture says – "The tablets are the work of God and the writing is God's
*writing, engraved on the tablets" (*SHEMOT 32:16*). Read not engraved*
[harut] but freedom [herut], for there is none who is free save one who is
occupied with Torah study. And anyone who is occupied with Torah study
will be exalted, as it is said – "And from God's gift [mattana] to God's heritage
[nahaliel] and from God's heritage [nahaliel] to high places [bamot] . . ."
(BEMIDBAR 21:19–20).

This statement points to the great deficit of those who reject the Torah,
and whose behavior is less than exemplary.

Such behavior within marriage prevents the marriage from being a
sacred and transcending reality. At worst, it may propel the marriage
into a harmful and painful relationship; devoid of caring, full of neglect,
and even abuse.

In the larger sense, failure to live up to one's sacred obligations
in marriage is a distinct form of abuse – abuse of privilege, abuse of
opportunity, abuse of responsibility, all under the heading of abuse
of one's marriage partner. All this is deserving of the most serious
rebuke.

The true exercise of freedom is not when a person does what they feel like doing. That is not freedom. That is caving in to narcissistic, self-serving wants.

True freedom, true humaneness, is realized through not letting anything get in the way of living up to one's undertakings.

The free person is the one who is not governed or enslaved by passions or cravings, and is instead free to act with care and dedication to the other. That is where exaltation, the *high places*, resides.

❧ MISHNAH 3 ❧

ג. הַלּוֹמֵד מֵחֲבֵרוֹ פֶּרֶק אֶחָד, אוֹ הֲלָכָה אַחַת, אוֹ פָּסוּק אֶחָד, אוֹ דִּבּוּר
אֶחָד, אוֹ אֲפִילוּ אוֹת אַחַת, צָרִיךְ לִנְהָג בּוֹ כָּבוֹד, שֶׁכֵּן מָצִינוּ בְּדָוִד מֶלֶךְ
יִשְׂרָאֵל, שֶׁלֹּא לָמַד מֵאֲחִיתֹפֶל אֶלָּא שְׁנֵי דְבָרִים בִּלְבַד, קְרָאוֹ רַבּוֹ אַלּוּפוֹ
וּמְיֻדָּעוֹ, שֶׁנֶּאֱמַר: וְאַתָּה אֱנוֹשׁ כְּעֶרְכִּי, אַלּוּפִי וּמְיֻדָּעִי. וַהֲלֹא דְבָרִים קַל
וָחֹמֶר - וּמַה דָּוִד מֶלֶךְ יִשְׂרָאֵל שֶׁלֹּא לָמַד מֵאֲחִיתֹפֶל אֶלָּא שְׁנֵי דְבָרִים
בִּלְבַד, קְרָאוֹ רַבּוֹ אַלּוּפוֹ וּמְיֻדָּעוֹ, הַלּוֹמֵד מֵחֲבֵרוֹ פֶּרֶק אֶחָד, אוֹ הֲלָכָה
אַחַת, אוֹ פָּסוּק אֶחָד, אוֹ דִּבּוּר אֶחָד, אוֹ אֲפִילוּ אוֹת אֶחָת, עַל אַחַת כַּמָּה
וְכַמָּה שֶׁצָּרִיךְ לִנְהָג בּוֹ כָּבוֹד. וְאֵין כָּבוֹד אֶלָּא תוֹרָה, שֶׁנֶּאֱמַר: כָּבוֹד חֲכָמִים
יִנְחָלוּ, וּתְמִימִים יִנְחֲלוּ טוֹב. וְאֵין טוֹב אֶלָּא תוֹרָה, שֶׁנֶּאֱמַר: כִּי לֶקַח טוֹב
נָתַתִּי לָכֶם, תּוֹרָתִי אַל תַּעֲזֹבוּ.

One who learns from a fellow a chapter, a law, a verse, an expression, or even a single letter, must behave toward that fellow with honor, as this is what we find concerning David King of Israel, who learned only two things from Ahisofel, yet he called him his master, his guide, and his beloved, as it is said – "But it was you, my equal, my guide, and my beloved" (TEHILLIM 55:14). *Is this not a logical derivation – if David, King of Israel, who learned only two things from Ahisofel, yet called him his master, his guide, and his beloved, how much more so that one who learns from a fellow a chapter, a law, a verse, an expression, or even a single letter, ought to behave toward that fellow with honor. Honor inheres in naught except the Torah, as it is said – "The wise shall inherit honor ..."* (MISHLAY 3:35) *"... and the wholehearted shall inherit good"* (MISHLAY 28:10). *And the good is naught but the Torah, as it is said – "For I have given you a good teaching, do not forsake My Torah"* (MISHLAY 4:2).

One can learn in many ways. One can learn from teachers, one can learn from study of text, and one can learn from example.

In marriage, learning from one's spouse is more than possible. It is ideal.

Each of the marital partners has their own unique strengths, such as patience, understanding, caring, generosity, helpfulness, etc.

All of these are hallowed virtues that are essential for marriage to flourish.

The one who excels in these and other virtues will likely teach the other by sheer force of example, and thereby make the other an even better person.

That is reason enough to be full of gratitude to one's spouse; to not only love one's spouse, but also to venerate one's spouse.

❧ MISHNAH 4 ❧

ד. כָּךְ הִיא דַּרְכָּהּ שֶׁל תּוֹרָה: פַּת בְּמֶלַח תֹּאכֵל, וּמַיִם בִּמְשׂוּרָה תִּשְׁתֶּה,
וְעַל הָאָרֶץ תִּישָׁן, וְחַיֵּי צַעַר תִּחְיֶה, וּבַתּוֹרָה אַתָּה עָמֵל. אִם אַתָּה עוֹשֶׂה
כֵּן, אַשְׁרֶיךָ וְטוֹב לָךְ – אַשְׁרֶיךָ בָּעוֹלָם הַזֶּה, וְטוֹב לָךְ לָעוֹלָם הַבָּא.

*This is the way of the Torah: that you eat bread with salt, drink water by
ration, sleep upon the ground, and live a life of hardship, and yet you toil
in the Torah. If you do this, "you will be happy and it will be well with you"
(TEHILLIM 128:2); you will be happy – in this world; and it will be well
with you – in the world-to-come.*

It is not wealth, or even a level of comfort, that brings marital happiness.

A happy couple are happy because they are a couple, united in
unconditional love and dedication to each other no matter the circumstance.

Toiling together to achieve the life mission even in the face of
hardship is the firm foundation for a solid marital union.

✤ MISHNAH 5 ✤

ה. אַל תְּבַקֵּשׁ גְּדֻלָּה לְעַצְמְךָ, וְאַל תַּחְמוֹד כָּבוֹד. יוֹתֵר מִלִּמּוּדֶךָ עֲשֵׂה, וְאַל תִּתְאַוֶּה לְשֻׁלְחָנָם שֶׁל מְלָכִים, שֶׁשֻּׁלְחָנְךָ גָּדוֹל מִשֻּׁלְחָנָם, וְכִתְרְךָ גָּדוֹל מִכִּתְרָם, וְנֶאֱמָן הוּא בַּעַל מְלַאכְתְּךָ שֶׁיְשַׁלֶּם לְךָ שְׂכַר פְּעֻלָּתֶךָ.

Do not seek greatness for yourself and do not covet honor. Let your deeds exceed your learning, and do not crave for the table of kings, for your table is greater than their table, and your crown greater than their crown, and trustworthy is your Employer to pay you the reward of your work.

A couple who are dedicated to each other will almost by definition fulfill each other. There would be no reason to covet anything when one has everything.

Even the idea that those who have fancier abodes or more important positions are happier because of that, is not true.

The crown of mutual and transcending love is greater than any other crown, royal or otherwise.

❧ MISHNAH 6 ❧

ו. גְּדוֹלָה תוֹרָה יוֹתֵר מִן הַכְּהֻנָּה וּמִן הַמַּלְכוּת, שֶׁהַמַּלְכוּת נִקְנֵית בִּשְׁלֹשִׁים מַעֲלוֹת וְהַכְּהֻנָּה בְּעֶשְׂרִים וְאַרְבַּע, וְהַתּוֹרָה נִקְנֵית בְּאַרְבָּעִים וּשְׁמוֹנָה דְבָרִים. וְאֵלּוּ הֵן: בְּתַלְמוּד, בִּשְׁמִיעַת הָאֹזֶן, בַּעֲרִיכַת שְׂפָתַיִם, בְּבִינַת הַלֵּב, בְּאֵימָה, בְּיִרְאָה, בַּעֲנָוָה, בְּשִׂמְחָה, בְּשִׁמּוּשׁ חֲכָמִים, בְּדִבּוּק חֲבֵרִים, בְּפִלְפּוּל הַתַּלְמִידִים, בְּיִשּׁוּב, בְּמִקְרָא, בְּמִשְׁנָה, בְּמִעוּט סְחוֹרָה, בְּמִעוּט דֶּרֶךְ אֶרֶץ, בְּמִעוּט תַּעֲנוּג, בְּמִעוּט שֵׁנָה, בְּמִעוּט שִׂיחָה, בְּמִעוּט שְׂחוֹק, בְּאֶרֶךְ אַפַּיִם, בְּלֵב טוֹב, בֶּאֱמוּנַת חֲכָמִים, בְּקַבָּלַת הַיִּסּוּרִין, הַמַּכִּיר אֶת מְקוֹמוֹ, וְהַשָּׂמֵחַ בְּחֶלְקוֹ, וְהָעוֹשֶׂה סְיָג לִדְבָרָיו, וְאֵינוֹ מַחֲזִיק טוֹבָה לְעַצְמוֹ, אָהוּב, אוֹהֵב אֶת הַמָּקוֹם, אוֹהֵב אֶת הַבְּרִיּוֹת, אוֹהֵב אֶת הַצְּדָקוֹת, אוֹהֵב אֶת הַמֵּישָׁרִים, אוֹהֵב אֶת הַתּוֹכָחוֹת, וּמִתְרַחֵק מִן הַכָּבוֹד, וְלֹא מֵגִיס לִבּוֹ בְּתַלְמוּדוֹ, וְאֵינוֹ שָׂמֵחַ בְּהוֹרָאָה, נוֹשֵׂא בְעֹל עִם חֲבֵרוֹ, וּמַכְרִיעוֹ לְכַף זְכוּת, וּמַעֲמִידוֹ עַל הָאֱמֶת, וּמַעֲמִידוֹ עַל הַשָּׁלוֹם, וּמִתְיַשֵּׁב לִבּוֹ בְּתַלְמוּדוֹ, שׁוֹאֵל וּמֵשִׁיב, שׁוֹמֵעַ וּמוֹסִיף, הַלּוֹמֵד עַל מְנָת לְלַמֵּד, וְהַלּוֹמֵד עַל מְנָת לַעֲשׂוֹת, הַמַּחְכִּים אֶת רַבּוֹ, וְהַמְכַוֵּן אֶת שְׁמוּעָתוֹ, וְהָאוֹמֵר דָּבָר בְּשֵׁם אוֹמְרוֹ. הָא לָמַדְתָּ, כָּל הָאוֹמֵר דָּבָר בְּשֵׁם אוֹמְרוֹ, מֵבִיא גְאֻלָּה לָעוֹלָם, שֶׁנֶּאֱמַר: וַתֹּאמֶר אֶסְתֵּר לַמֶּלֶךְ בְּשֵׁם מָרְדְּכָי.

Greater is Torah than priesthood and kingship, for kingship is achieved through thirty virtues and the priesthood through twenty-four, but the Torah is acquired through forty-eight virtues. They are: 1) by study; 2) by attentive listening; 3) by proper enunciation; 4) by an understanding and perceptive heart; 5) by reverence; 6) by awe; 7) by humility; 8) by joy; 9) by ministering to sages; 10) by attaching oneself to colleagues; 11) by keen discussion among students; 12) by calm deliberation; 13) by study of scripture; 14) by study of Mishnah; 15) by moderating business activity; 16) by moderating involvement in worldly matters; 17) by moderating pleasure; 18) by moderating sleep; 19) by moderating idle chatter; 20) by moderating jest; 21) by being slow to anger; 22) by having a good heart; 23) by trusting in the sages; 24) by acceptance of affliction; 25) by recognizing one's place; 26) by rejoicing in one's portion; 27) by putting a guard to one's words; 28) by not claiming merit for one's self; 29) by being beloved; 30) by loving God; 31) by loving humankind; 32) by loving acts of charity; 33) by loving *rectitude; 34) by loving reproof; 35) by keeping distant from honor; 36) by not boasting of one's learning; 37) by not enjoying handing down decisions; 38) by sharing burdens with one's fellow; 39) by judging one's fellow charitably; 40) by leading one's fellow to truth; 41) by leading one's fellow to peace; 42) by being studious in learning; 43) by asking and answering, listening and adding to knowledge; 44) by learning in order to teach; 45) by learning in order to practice; 46) by enhancing the wisdom of one's teacher; 47) by being exact in what one has learned; and 48) by reporting a statement in the name of its author. For thus have you learned – whoever reports a statement in the name of its author brings deliverance to the world, as it is said – "and Esther told it to the king in Mordekhai's name"* (ESTHER 2:22).

Applied to marriage, these forty-eight virtues lead to marital excellence.

The Torah for marriage includes these virtues. 1. *Study* – to learn how to be a responsible marital partner. 2. *Attentive listening* – listening carefully and thereby knowing more completely. 3. *Proper enunciation* – verbalizing what one has learned so that it is more likely to be implemented. 4. *An understanding and perceptive heart* – to integrate Torah values into the marriage, one must have the heart in it; i.e., the desire to excel. 5. *Reverence* – to revere the teacher of the Torah values. 6. *Awe* – to be in awe of the values themselves. 7. *Humility* – the natural result of the reverence and awe is humility in the face of the task – to effect a harmonious marriage. 8. *Joy* – to approach marriage in joy at having this sacred opportunity. 9. *Ministering to sages* – to continue, in humility, to learn. 10. *Attaching oneself to colleagues* – from whom one gains contemporaneous perspective. 11. *Keen discussion among students* – which is an even more robust way to entrench one's knowledge. 12. *Calm deliberation* – thereby avoiding the rush to wrong conclusions. 13. *Study of scripture* – a most necessary reinforcement of Torah values. 14. *Study of Mishnah* – and the application of these Torah values through the insights of the sages. 15. *Moderating business activity* – business activity to look after the home is necessary, but too much, thereby taking away from the home, is ill-advised. 16. *Moderating involvement in worldly matters* – here too, deflection from placing primacy on the home detracts from the marriage. 17. *Moderating plea-sure* – pleasure is important in the marital union, but in moderation so as to avoid abuse. 18. *Moderating sleep* – enough sleep is needed, but too much injects laziness where energy is needed. 19. *Moderating idle chatter* – needless talk has its place, but too much is out of place, and demeaning. 20. *Moderating jest* – there is room for jokes and banter, but not at the expense of the seriousness of the marriage. 21. *Being slow to anger* – anger is a destructive force in the relationship, and even the fear of eruption disturbs marital harmony. 22. *Having a good heart* – and thereby seeking ways of being a helpful and caring marital partner. 23. *Trusting in the sages* – that their advice regarding marital harmony is rooted in the full understanding of marital togetherness. 24. *Acceptance of affliction* – such that if there are difficulties, the relationship is not punctuated with blame, and is instead strengthened by the resolve to address matters together with loving dedication. 25. *Recognizing one's place* – and therefore understanding what is one's responsibility in challenging situations. 26. *Rejoicing in one's portion* – and totally and happily embracing one's partner. 27. *Putting a guard to one's words* – so that one does not inadvertently blurt out words that are hurtful. 28. *Not claiming merit for one's self* – and instead doing what is proper because it is the correct way to act, without looking to be praised. 29. *Being beloved* – by doing things that escalate the love and adulation of one's spouse. 30. *Loving God* – and thereby being more appreciative of one's marital blessing. 31. *Loving humankind* – since loving in general is more likely to foster a loving personality. 32. *Loving acts of charity* – and by being kind, kindness becomes a natural part of one's being, making the kind person a better marriage partner. 33. *Loving rectitude* – and thus, rather than imposing one's own idea of what is needed in a specific situation, one is more sensi-tive to what the other needs, and is alert to protecting their dignity. 34. *Loving reproof* – as a welcome way to sincerely wanting to do better. 35. *Keeping distant from honor* – is more likely to occur when one bestows honor on one's spouse, and feels uplifted by so doing. 36. *Not boasting of one's learning* – and instead seeing the learning as essential to living properly. 37. *Not enjoying handing down decisions* – thereby avoiding being judgmental and critical. 38. *Sharing burdens with one's fellow* – and thereby strengthening the marital union. 39. *Judging one's fellow charitably* – and not attributing bad motives to the spouse's failing. 40. *Leading one's fellow to truth* – which is better attained through gentle and mutual interaction. 41. *Leading one's fellow to peace* – through working together to achieve harmony. 42. *Being studious in learning* – after all the attainments, to not let laxity set in, and instead to look for more ways to excel in the union. 43. *Asking and answering, listening and adding to knowledge* – from one's spouse, which is sure to uncover more ways to enhance the marriage. 44. *Learning in order to teach* – and share with one's marriage partner. 45. *Learning in order to practice* – which thereby escalates the knowledge up a few notches as it improves the marital reality. 46. *Enhancing the wisdom of one's teacher* – by being an exemplar worth emulating. 47. *Being exact in what one has learned* – because there should be no short cuts or mis-interpretations in addressing one's marital obligations. 48. *Reporting a statement in the name of its author* – and if the author is one's spouse, ultimately being proud of one's spouse in a way that inspires others to emulate such admiration.

❧ MISHNAH 7 ❧

ז. גְּדוֹלָה תוֹרָה, שֶׁהִיא נוֹתֶנֶת חַיִּים לְעֹשֶׁיהָ בָּעוֹלָם הַזֶּה וּבָעוֹלָם הַבָּא,
שֶׁנֶּאֱמַר: כִּי חַיִּים הֵם לְמוֹצְאֵיהֶם, וּלְכָל בְּשָׂרוֹ מַרְפֵּא. וְאוֹמֵר: רְפְאוּת תְּהִי
לְשָׁרֶּךָ, וְשִׁקּוּי לְעַצְמוֹתֶיךָ. וְאוֹמֵר: עֵץ חַיִּים הִיא לַמַּחֲזִיקִים בָּהּ, וְתוֹמְכֶיהָ
מְאֻשָּׁר. וְאוֹמֵר: כִּי לִוְיַת חֵן הֵם לְרֹאשֶׁךָ וַעֲנָקִים לְגַרְגְּרֹתֶיךָ. וְאוֹמֵר: תִּתֵּן
לְרֹאשְׁךָ לִוְיַת חֵן, עֲטֶרֶת תִּפְאֶרֶת תְּמַגְּנֶךָּ. וְאוֹמֵר: כִּי בִי יִרְבּוּ יָמֶיךָ, וְיוֹסִיפוּ
לְךָ שְׁנוֹת חַיִּים. וְאוֹמֵר: אֹרֶךְ יָמִים בִּימִינָהּ, בִּשְׂמֹאלָהּ עֹשֶׁר וְכָבוֹד. וְאוֹמֵר:
כִּי אֹרֶךְ יָמִים וּשְׁנוֹת חַיִּים וְשָׁלוֹם יוֹסִיפוּ לָךְ.

*Great is the Torah, for it brings life to those who practice it, in this world
and in the world-to-come, as it is said – "For they are life to those who find
them and health to all their flesh" (MISHLAY 4:22); and it says – "It is a tree
of life to those who maintain it and those who support it are praiseworthy"
(MISHLAY 3:18); and it says – "They shall be a garland of grace for your
head, and necklaces around your neck" (MISHLAY 1:9); and it says – "It
gives to your head a garland of grace, and will bestow upon you a crown of
glory" (MISHLAY 4:9); and it says – "For through Me the number of your
days will grow, and the years of your life will be increased" (MISHLAY 9:11);
and it says – "Length of days is at its right, at its left are riches and honor"
(MISHLAY 3:16); and it says – "For length of days and years of life and peace
will they add to you" (MISHLAY 3:2).*

Applying Torah regulations and values to marriage, infusing marriage
with abiding love, respect, honor, caring, and devotion, gives the
marriage life and vibrancy in this world, and lasts for eternity.

❧ MISHNAH 8 ❧

ח. רַבִּי שִׁמְעוֹן בֶּן יְהוּדָה מִשּׁוּם רַבִּי שִׁמְעוֹן בֶּן יוֹחָאי אוֹמֵר: הַנּוֹי, וְהַכֹּחַ,
וְהָעֹשֶׁר, וְהַכָּבוֹד, וְהַחָכְמָה, וְהַזִּקְנָה, וְהַשֵּׂיבָה, וְהַבָּנִים, נָאֶה לַצַּדִּיקִים וְנָאֶה
לָעוֹלָם, שֶׁנֶּאֱמַר: עֲטֶרֶת תִּפְאֶרֶת שֵׂיבָה, בְּדֶרֶךְ צְדָקָה תִּמָּצֵא. וְאוֹמֵר:
תִּפְאֶרֶת בַּחוּרִים כֹּחָם, וַהֲדַר זְקֵנִים שֵׂיבָה. וְאוֹמֵר: עֲטֶרֶת זְקֵנִים בְּנֵי בָנִים,
וְתִפְאֶרֶת בָּנִים אֲבוֹתָם. וְאוֹמֵר: וְחָפְרָה הַלְּבָנָה וּבוֹשָׁה הַחַמָּה, כִּי מָלַךְ
יְיָ צְבָאוֹת בְּהַר צִיּוֹן וּבִירוּשָׁלַיִם, וְנֶגֶד זְקֵנָיו כָּבוֹד. רַבִּי שִׁמְעוֹן בֶּן מְנַסְיָא
אוֹמֵר: אֵלּוּ שֶׁבַע מִדּוֹת שֶׁמָּנוּ חֲכָמִים לַצַּדִּיקִים, כֻּלָּם נִתְקַיְמוּ בְּרַבִּי וּבְבָנָיו.

Rabbe Shimon the son of Yehuda, in the name of Rabbe Shimon the son of Yohai, says: Beauty, strength, riches, honor, wisdom, old-age, fullness of years, and children, are becoming to the righteous and becoming to the world, as it is said – "Fullness of years is a crown of glory, it is found in the path of righteousness" (MISHLAY 16:31); and it says – "The glory of the young is their strength and the beauty of the old is in the fullness of their years" (MISHLAY 20:29); and it says – "The crown of the wise is their riches . . ." (MISHLAY 14:24); and it says – "The crown of the old is grandchildren, and the glory of children is their parents" (MISHLAY 17:6); and it says – "The moon will be confounded and the sun ashamed, for the Lord of Hosts will reign in Mount Zion and in Jerusalem, and God's elders shall meet honor" (YESHAYAHU 24:23). Rabbe Shimon the son of Menasya says: These seven attributes enumerated by the sages for the righteous, all were realized in Rabbe [Yehuda haNasi] and his sons.

Lest one think that the embrace of Torah precludes having beauty, riches, and honor, here we are told to the contrary. Even more, these seemingly material items are interspersed with strength, wisdom, old-age and fullness of years, and children.

These are all becoming to the righteous, as the righteous know how to integrate all these realities into the entirety of life.

The righteous will not waste their wealth on nonsense, nor their strength on unimportant endeavors, nor their beauty on vain pursuits, nor their honor on seeking more glory.

Instead, over the span over a meaningful life, they will wisely expend their energy and their largesse on making the world a better place, and bequeath that legacy to their children, as was indeed the case with Rabbe Yehuda haNasi, who compiled the very treatise herein being studied.

In the wrong hands, some of these blessings can easily be distorted. For a righteous couple who have these blessings, it is becoming to them, and a precious, enduring lesson in how to live.

❧ MISHNAH 9 ❧

ט. אָמַר רַבִּי יוֹסֵי בֶּן קִסְמָא: פַּעַם אַחַת הָיֵיתִי מְהַלֵּךְ בַּדֶּרֶךְ, וּפָגַע בִּי אָדָם אֶחָד, וְנָתַן לִי שָׁלוֹם, וְהֶחֱזַרְתִּי לוֹ שָׁלוֹם. אָמַר לִי: רַבִּי, מֵאֵיזֶה מָקוֹם אָתָּה. אָמַרְתִּי לוֹ: מֵעִיר גְּדוֹלָה שֶׁל חֲכָמִים וְשֶׁל סוֹפְרִים אָנִי. אָמַר לִי: רַבִּי, רְצוֹנְךָ שֶׁתָּדוּר עִמָּנוּ בִּמְקוֹמֵנוּ, וַאֲנִי אֶתֵּן לְךָ אֶלֶף אַלְפִים דִּינְרֵי זָהָב וַאֲבָנִים טוֹבוֹת וּמַרְגָּלִיּוֹת. אָמַרְתִּי לוֹ: אִם אַתָּה נוֹתֵן לִי כָּל כֶּסֶף וְזָהָב וַאֲבָנִים טוֹבוֹת וּמַרְגָּלִיּוֹת שֶׁבָּעוֹלָם, אֵינִי דָר אֶלָּא בִּמְקוֹם תּוֹרָה, וְכֵן כָּתוּב בְּסֵפֶר תְּהִלִּים עַל יְדֵי דָוִד מֶלֶךְ יִשְׂרָאֵל: טוֹב לִי תוֹרַת פִּיךָ, מֵאַלְפֵי זָהָב וָכָסֶף. וְלֹא עוֹד, אֶלָּא שֶׁבִּשְׁעַת פְּטִירָתוֹ שֶׁל אָדָם, אֵין מְלַוִּין לוֹ לְאָדָם לֹא כֶסֶף וְלֹא זָהָב וְלֹא אֲבָנִים טוֹבוֹת וּמַרְגָּלִיּוֹת, אֶלָּא תוֹרָה וּמַעֲשִׂים טוֹבִים בִּלְבַד, שֶׁנֶּאֱמַר: בְּהִתְהַלֶּכְךָ תַּנְחֶה אֹתָךְ, בְּשָׁכְבְּךָ תִּשְׁמוֹר עָלֶיךָ, וַהֲקִיצוֹתָ הִיא תְשִׂיחֶךָ. בְּהִתְהַלֶּכְךָ תַּנְחֶה אֹתָךְ - בָּעוֹלָם הַזֶּה; בְּשָׁכְבְּךָ תִּשְׁמוֹר עָלֶיךָ - בַּקֶּבֶר; וַהֲקִיצוֹתָ הִיא תְשִׂיחֶךָ - לָעוֹלָם הַבָּא. וְאוֹמֵר: לִי הַכֶּסֶף וְלִי הַזָּהָב, נְאֻם יְיָ צְבָאוֹת.

Rabbe Yose the son of Kisma said: Once I was walking on the road, and was met by a certain person who greeted me, and I returned the greeting. He said to me – "Rabbe, from what place are you?" I said to him – "I am from a great city of sages and scribes." He said to me – "Rabbe, if you are willing to live with us, I will give you a million golden dinar and precious stones and pearls." I said to him – "Even if you were to give to me all the silver and gold and precious stones and pearls in the world, I would not live anywhere except in a place imbued with Torah." And thus is it written in the Book of Psalms by David, King of Israel – "The Torah of your mouth is better for me than thousands of gold and silver" (TEHILLIM 119:72). *Moreover, when a person dies, neither silver nor gold nor precious stones and pearls accompany that person, only Torah and good deeds, as it is said – "When you walk it shall lead you, when you lie down it shall watch over you, and when you awaken it shall talk with you"* (MISHLAY 6:22). *When you walk it shall lead you – in this world; when you lie down it shall watch over you – in the grave; and when you awaken it shall talk with you – in the world-to-come. And it says – "Mine is the silver and Mine is the gold, says the Lord of Hosts"* (HAGGAI 2:8).

Having just been told that wealth is befitting to the righteous, this story seems to contradict that very message.

Rabbe Yose refuses the offer to move to a city for a huge sum of money. He prefers to remain where he is, a place imbued with Torah.

Actually, with all that money Rabbe Yose could have built a Torah imbued city. But he turned down this magnanimous offer. Why?

Perhaps Rabbe Yose strongly preferred a place wherein the Torah values were primary, not where the money came first and would be the ostensible reason why people move there.

In effect, this story is not contradictory at all. It places the matter of wealth into true perspective. Wealth is becoming, fitting, and necessary, financial capacity can be put to good use; but that is secondary to the more primary, value-laden life we are urged to live.

The couple who are blessed with financial bounty are best served when that bounty is subordinated to the more primary focus on a home suffused with Torah values.

❧ MISHNAH 10 ❧

י. חֲמִשָּׁה קִנְיָנִים קָנָה לוֹ הַקָּדוֹשׁ בָּרוּךְ הוּא בְּעוֹלָמוֹ, וְאֵלּוּ הֵן: תּוֹרָה קִנְיָן אֶחָד, שָׁמַיִם וָאָרֶץ קִנְיָן אֶחָד, אַבְרָהָם קִנְיָן אֶחָד, יִשְׂרָאֵל קִנְיָן אֶחָד, בֵּית הַמִּקְדָּשׁ קִנְיָן אֶחָד. תּוֹרָה מִנַּיִן, דִּכְתִיב: ה' קָנָנִי רֵאשִׁית דַּרְכּוֹ קֶדֶם מִפְעָלָיו מֵאָז. שָׁמַיִם וָאָרֶץ קִנְיָן אֶחָד מִנַּיִן, דִּכְתִיב: כֹּה אָמַר ה' הַשָּׁמַיִם כִּסְאִי וְהָאָרֶץ הֲדֹם רַגְלָי אֵי זֶה בַיִת אֲשֶׁר תִּבְנוּ לִי וְאֵי זֶה מָקוֹם מְנוּחָתִי; וְאוֹמֵר מָה רַבּוּ מַעֲשֶׂיךָ ה' כֻּלָּם בְּחָכְמָה עָשִׂיתָ מָלְאָה הָאָרֶץ קִנְיָנֶךָ. אַבְרָהָם קִנְיָן אֶחָד מִנַּיִן, דִּכְתִיב: וַיְבָרְכֵהוּ וַיֹּאמַר בָּרוּךְ אַבְרָם לְאֵל עֶלְיוֹן קֹנֵה שָׁמַיִם וָאָרֶץ. יִשְׂרָאֵל קִנְיָן אֶחָד מִנַּיִן, דִּכְתִיב: עַד יַעֲבֹר עַמְּךָ ה' עַד יַעֲבֹר עַם זוּ קָנִיתָ; וְאוֹמֵר לִקְדוֹשִׁים אֲשֶׁר בָּאָרֶץ הֵמָּה וְאַדִּירֵי כָּל חֶפְצִי בָם. בֵּית הַמִּקְדָּשׁ קִנְיָן אֶחָד מִנַּיִן, דִּכְתִיב: מָכוֹן לְשִׁבְתְּךָ פָּעַלְתָּ ה' מִקְדָּשׁ ה' כּוֹנְנוּ יָדֶיךָ; וְאוֹמֵר וַיְבִיאֵם אֶל גְּבוּל קָדְשׁוֹ הַר זֶה קָנְתָה יְמִינוֹ.

*Five acquisitions did the Holy One, blessed is God, acquire for God in God's world. They are: The Torah – one acquisition; heaven and earth – one acquisition; Avraham – one acquisition; Israel – one acquisition; the Holy Sanctuary – one acquisition. How is this derived concerning the Torah? Because it is written – "God acquired me as the beginning of God's way, before all of God's work from of old" (*MISHLAY 8:22*). How is this derived concerning heaven and earth? Because it is written – "Thus says God: The heaven is My throne and the earth is My footstool, what type of house will you build for Me and what type of place for My rest" (*YESHAYAHU 66:1*); and it says – "How manifold are Your works, God, all of them You made in wisdom, the earth is full of Your acquisitions" (*TEHILLIM 104:24*). How is this derived concerning Avraham? Because it is written – "And he blessed him, saying – blessed be Avram to the Most-High God, Acquirer of heaven and earth" (*BERESHIS 14:19*). How is this derived concerning Israel? Because it is written – "until your people pass over, God, until this nation You have acquired passes over" (*SHEMOS 15:16*); and it says – "For the holy who are in the earth, they are the noble through whom all My will is done" (*TEHILLIM 16:3*). How is this derived concerning the Holy Sanctuary? Because it is written – "the place, God, You have prepared for You to dwell in, the Sanctuary, God, which Your hands have established" (*SHEMOS 15:17*); and it is said – "And God brought them to God's sacred boundary, to this mountain, that God's right hand had acquired" (*TEHILLIM 78:54*).*

The Torah, heaven and earth, Avraham, Israel, and the Holy Sanctuary – all acquisitions of God?

Really! These were all made possible by God. God gave us the Torah, God created heaven and earth, God gave us Avraham, God embraced Israel, and God made the Holy Sanctuary possible.

In what way are these God's acquisitions? This is surely not about acquisition in the "property rights" sense.

Perhaps the message here is that God took ownership of all these as God's special projects.

The Hebrew word employed here to denote acquisition is *kinyan,* the word that is used in describing this chapter – Kinyan Torah, acquiring the Torah. It does not mean purchase; it means taking ownership of the Torah as our guide.

Kinyan is likewise employed as part of the legal process of marrying. It is not buying one's wife; it is taking ownership of the responsibility for one's wife.

Getting married is a legal undertaking, in a similar sense to God's acquisitions. It is the embrace of a sublime responsibility, as serious as a contractual obligation. The foundation is legal; carrying out the obligation is a profound expression of love.

❧ MISHNAH 11 ❧

יא. כָּל מַה שֶּׁבָּרָא הַקָּדוֹשׁ בָּרוּךְ הוּא בְּעוֹלָמוֹ, לֹא בְרָאוֹ אֶלָּא לִכְבוֹדוֹ,
שֶׁנֶּאֱמַר: כֹּל הַנִּקְרָא בִשְׁמִי וְלִכְבוֹדִי, בְּרָאתִיו יְצַרְתִּיו אַף עֲשִׂיתִיו. וְאוֹמֵר:
יְיָ יִמְלֹךְ לְעֹלָם וָעֶד.

*Whatever the Holy One, blessed is God, created in God's world, God created
solely for God's glory, as it is said – "All that is called by My Name and that I
have created for My glory, I have formed, even made"* (YESHAYAHU 43:7);
and it says – "God shall reign for all eternity" (SHEMOS 15:18).

Does God need glory; to the extent that this was the basis and rationale
for creation?

What exactly do we mean by God's glory? How exactly is God
glorified?

In a word, when we live by God's word, by God's Torah, and we
do so in letter and spirit, we thereby glorify God in the eyes of others,
and inspire them by our example.

We inspire them to reach upward, and behave in a way that is
unique to humans – with care, with compassion, with generosity,
with kindness, with all that is takes to overwhelm the world with
goodness.

God wants this glory because this is how humans justify and
ennoble creation.

Applying all these wonderful human capacities to marriage, applying Pirkay Avos to marriage – it does not get more glorious than
that.